Being Miss Behaved

◆

Nancy
to a wonderful
life long friends
Catharine

Being Miss Behaved

Humorous Essays for the Politically Incorrect

◆

Catharine Bramkamp

Writers Club Press
San Jose New York Lincoln Shanghai

Being Miss Behaved
Humorous Essays for the Politically Incorrect

Writers Club Press
an imprint of iUniverse.com, Inc.

For information address:
iUniverse.com, Inc.
5220 S 16th, Ste. 200
Lincoln, NE 68512
www.iuniverse.com

ISBN: 0-595-18570-3

Printed in the United States of America

To my parents who read Eloise to me
when I was young and impressionable.

And to my husband,
who is not Miss Behaved at all.

Contents

◆

Cross Children Walk

Travelers Tales Out of Turn

Tea and Sympathy

Introduction

───────────── ◆ ─────────────

Bubbles, Early Miss Behaved

As a child I experienced the elderly in two different ways; traditional, where I had to sit quietly for about a century or so with nothing to eat but these cookies that had a strange almond taste and listen to my mother make pleasant comments about the weather and remind me not to touch the precious collection of porcelain dogs on the low table and Miss Behaved. At the time I didn't realize how wonderful the second choice was in terms of being 80 years old, but to quote an often quote poem, the last chapter in a Miss Behaved life is very purple.

Her name was Elaine, but as a baby she produced so many magnificent bubbles on such a consistent basis that she was called Bubbles. The name stuck for the rest of her life. It suited her. She was a small, round woman with a twinkle of mischief (hers, ours, anyone in town who was raising hell, it was all entertaining) in her blue eyes.

Every visit to Bubble's house was an occasion. Even as a child, I had the run of the house and could touch as many things as I pleased because the prevailing attitude was they were just things. Things were meant to be touched.

"Go get some wine", Bubbles told me. "It's five o'clock somewhere."

She kept all the wine in her refrigerator—a vintage 50s affair— short, round and pink in a world filled with big white, square General Electric models. I had seen other old-lady refrigerators; this has the most personality both outside and inside.

Instead of the expected rows of Metamucil bottles in varying stages of expiration, tall bottles of laxatives, short bottles of vitamin supplements, bottles of strangely colored liquid that had to be taken two-and-a-half-hours, (one hour before but no later than two hours after eating) I encountered tiny bottles of Sutter Home White Zinfandel and larger bottles of Nevada City Table Red. The top shelf held no medicine at all but was cluttered with half used bags of chocolate chips, nuts, candies, and rectangle cubes of real butter.

Pink on the outside, garnished with magnets donated by devoted nephews and nieces, and non-conformist on the inside, it was my first inkling that refrigerators could actually reflect the inner life of the soul. A Miss Behaved concept to be sure.

She didn't change, but I did. When I had my own children, who were disinclined to sit still and admire glass objects from a distance while nibbling on snacks of stale crackers they didn't particularly care for, she still insisted on meeting them.

The first thing my two boys did was attempt to push each other through the cat door.

She laughed and bade them good luck.

Instead of an enormous paint-by-numbers family portrait on the wall, she displayed two California license plates, two different years, same number. Number four. Her father owned the first car in Nevada County and secured California license number four, the Governor, in nearby Sacramento owned the third car in the state and held license number three. Many had offered money for those plates, well before eBay. She refused them all. She liked her license plates, their history, and the way they balanced the fifty pounds of newspapers and magazines stacked against the wall.

Her stack wasn't a fiercely guarded fire hazard started during the war effort and not moved since. These newspapers were recent editions of the *Chronicle* and the *Wall Street Journal*. She read both every day. She asked my opinion about current events, then asked my mother. She already knew about the weather; she was interested in the different opinions of different generations. She, who never lived anywhere else but Nevada City, considered much of what goes on in the world very foolish, but she followed the news anyway. She thought Jerry Springer was just appalling. She was shocked every time she watched the show.

She was unfailingly cheerful, happy in her life, and full of delightful gossip, because everyone in town liked to talk and visit with her. She repeated everything from one informant to another. It wasn't until she was gone that residents of Nevada City realized they needed DSL. Up to that point, information flowed quite freely and quickly.

I've read about Miss Behaved older women, like Emily Carr, the artist who would push her monkey down the streets of Victoria in a baby carriage. She was very Miss Behaved in a big show-off way.

Bubbles was more quiet; she lived an under-the–radar Miss Behaved life. She did exactly as she pleased and was satisfied with the range of her powers and influence. She was calmly Miss Behaved. She served children Chips Ahoy cookies right before their dinner and offered wine at three in the afternoon. She'd sneak in her own little flask of brandy to the annual Women's Club Tea, then tell everyone what she was doing. She shared her daily papers, "Take a *Wall Street Journal* home. There's a story in there about unwed mothers, but let me tell you about Susie down the street...."

There is no question that there are profound benefits to substituting medicine with cookies. In her memory I purchase real butter, bags of chocolate chips, and bottles of wine. I will always be grateful for that first glimpse of the Miss Behaved joy of impropriety, the delight in shucking all the rules.

Miss Behaved people are not serious. Miss Behaved people do everything wrong, indulge in ludicrously inappropriate scenarios and not only come out unscathed, but manage to have a good time in the process.

Some afternoon you may discover, to your surprise, that you really wanted to spend your only two-week vacation in the Caribbean rather than schlepping the kids to the annual five generation family reunion in Missouri. You may suddenly wish to act upon a passing fancy to dye yours and the dog's hair red so you match. You may, one Monday morning, be overcome with the temptation to pour beer on your cereal.

Miss Behaved people recommend you do all of the above.

Bubbles showed me a better future, one of gossip and happy refrigerators. Being Miss Behaved is a collection of essays meant to offer guidance and inspiration for even the most unhappily correct among us.

Bubbles would approve.

Society At Large

Why Barbie is Miss Behaved

◆

Barbie's representation of what a person, or girl, should grow up to look like is her most lasting and Miss Behaved contribution to female society. What girl, well into her forties, doesn't harbor a sneaking suspicion that her breasts should really be rock hard and pointed? And what Miss Behaved woman hasn't, at one time or another, snuck into a plastic surgeon or two in search of those very dimensions? Just fill me in like Barbie is the common Miss Behaved request. Give me those lips, the permanent eyeliner, and five feet of leg length.

Miss Behaved women want to look like Barbie; they want to be Barbie; they love Barbie. This is why:

Barbie hangs in there at all cost. Since her invention, she has never left the shelves. There was that unfortunate incident with the Trailer Trash Barbie, a Barbie with dark roots and no fashion sense whatsoever. But Barbie, the icon and the ideal, survived such insubordination and came out the stronger for it by moving into her Fashions for Every Season phase. We like the London in Fall look ourselves. Barbie quietly found a new hairdresser, redid her roots, and moved on.

Barbie is independent. When Barbie vacations, it is with friends or alone. Barbie intuitively knows how to operate the Barbie barbecue; she always knows where she's headed in the Barbie RV; she does not have to take training to race the Barbie dirt bike or pilot the Barbie plane. Barbie camps with a single sleeping bag. When Barbie wanted to join the Coast Guard, or the *Bay Watch* team, did she need permission? Or even skills?

She did not; she just raced out and became part of whatever career fad appealed. We find it interesting that Businesswoman Barbie had a much shorter shelf life than *Bay Watch* Barbie, which should tell Miss Behaved career women something, but most chose to ignore the message.

Barbie is true to herself. Olympic Runner Barbie still owns the tiniest feet and biggest breasts in the toy kingdom. Barbie has not changed her body to fit into the next look or new era. Every year a writer or two protests that if Barbie was a real woman, she'd tip over. But, to Barbie, her proportions feel real enough and suit her lifestyle. In the seventies her proportions were changed, and we had, for a moment or two, the choice of Real Life Proportions Barbie. But no one bought the new look and that Barbie was quickly retired in favor of the original. Like the new Coke. Barbie's tenacity should be admired; despite her handlers, she never lost her figure or even misplaced it for more than a holiday season.

Barbie has a full life as a single woman even though she gets married all the time. She is the archetype bride without the bother of becoming a wife. When it's time to purchase a new bridal gown, a little something by Vera Wang, for instance, that needs to be seen in context, Ken is pulled out from the bottom drawer to stand up with Barbie. As soon as the ceremony is over and the photos have been taken, Ken is promptly consigned to the male oblivion that is required in Barbie's world. How do we know there is no coupled life after a Barbie wedding?

Consider the Barbie Mansion. The Barbie Mansion, or Townhouse depending on a girl's reference, is pink. The Barbie Bedroom Set features a pink and white four-poster canopied bed—every girl's fantasy, every man's nightmare. There is no garage attached to the Barbie house and thus there are no elemental garage accessories like a table saw and a beaten down orange and yellow couch that sits in the shadow of the open garage door. There is no Barbie weed-whacker.

Inside the typical Barbie house, there is no place for Ken at all. No paneled study, no Barbie big screen TV, no pink remote. No beer. Barbie does not need any of those things and there is no need to accommodate anyone else but herself. There may be no Barbie belt sander, but there is a Barbie closet with an electric clothing rack.

Remember that Barbie was the first celebrity to become a single mother on a consistently unapologetic basis. Years ago Barbie came complete with nursery furniture, baby clothes, rattles, bathing baby set, and a small baby— without the help of Ken. He was in the drawer the whole time. When Barbie wants a baby, she purchases a baby. Her long and stoic silence on the whereabouts of the father is the envy of stars like Madonna and Jodie Foster.

We know there are no co-parent Barbie sets. There are no happy-couple Barbies either. The couple sets that are displayed and promoted in Barbie's Miss Behaved world are Rhett and Scarlet and Scully and Mulder. And there is even an Elizabeth Taylor Barbie (without Richard Burton) dressed as Cleopatra or Maybe We Can Recover Some Of The Movie Cost in a Postmortem Licensing Agreement Barbie.

Barbie's computer is pink and she was the first to think of it.

Barbie is one of the fashion icons of the twentieth century and has advanced her art to the point that her clothing needs more support than the leads in Beach Blanket Babylon. She has advanced to the point where her most fabulous dresses are suspiciously grown up and only good for collecting. The other day, while admiring a Bob Mackie African Queen creation with a beaded collar that in real life would extend roughly three feet around Barbie's neck, there was some speculation as to how Barbie could eat her $1,000-a-plate charity dinner. But then we all realized that Barbie doesn't eat at those events. There are always photographers lurking around and a person is very unattractive while chewing.

Barbie is so resilient that even when she's poked, prodded or the dog buries her arm in the backyard, her expression never changes. She is unflappable, cool, and completely devoted to her mission of being the best-dressed doll with the most stuff in the playroom.

How could she not be the favorite Miss Behaved doll?

The Manly Man's Guide
to Dance Appreciation

◆

Dear Miss Behaved,

My wife has ballet tickets. Her best friend is sick. I'm next. Do you have any helpful Miss Behaved advice for me? And is the 't' silent or not?

Signed,

I thought White Oak was a Tree

Dear White,

A few superficially Miss Behaved people think they are fighting the good fight by drinking too many beers chased by one too many latte's (to create a bizarre equilibrium), then holding a belching contest in the restroom of Pac Bell park because the acoustics are so good. But like your wife, deeply and profoundly Miss Behaved people not only understand ballet, they pay good money for season tickets. This is a Miss Behaved thing to do because so few people understand dance in the first place, let alone understand why someone would pay good money to see men in tights cavort across the stage.

On the other hand, some people have no problem at all understanding why some people spend a great deal of money to watch men in tights cavort across the stage. Some people, in fact, take out home equity loans so they can sit very close to the stage.

But here you are, out of your element, out of your sweats and out 65 bucks.

And here is help.

First of all, do not panic. The ballet season begins after the Super Bowl has been played. Coincidence? We think not.

Second, remember ballet is more than mere entertainment. If we wanted to be amused, we'd stay at home and watch Cartoon Network. Ballet is about art; it has meaning. It requires appropriate seriousness and knowledge of the correct proprietary terms to describe the experience.

If you do not have the right words, or even a very large vocabulary, here are a few Miss Behaved survival tips.

The first thing to do is read the program notes. This information is critical if you accidentally fall asleep during the second program because Bach always puts you to sleep which is why your wife, realizing she married someone who is culturally backward, never takes you to these things in the first place. But remember this was an emergency. When she whacks you with a very hard and pointy Judith Lieber evening bag in the shape of a penguin, sit up straight and comment that the story line was weak. This is an especially good thing to say if the program was Jewels, because there is never a plot line in a Balanchine ballet. Or pretend you thought there was a plot because of the way the dancers kept leaning to the left and you're sensitive to that kind of symbolism.

During a classical ballet (see below for more information) when the hunter gestures to his best friend (the one in the lesser pair of tights with the smaller weapon), the hero is not saying, "You have something stuck in your teeth." He is saying, "That mysterious bird that I sense is really a young women held under an enchanted spell, has a beautiful face." In classical ballet there are no graceful pantomime gestures to express what a red blooded hunter is really admiring, especially since it could be his best friend, even if the best friend appears to have a small weapon.

Do be very serious. Don't laugh out loud, but you may chuckle knowingly when the ballerina lifts her arm a millimeter too high as an ironic tribute to Merce Cunningham.

Do not ask about the scoring system. There are no winners in art, except that you paid to watch them perform, which, after an evening of confusion on your part and sweat and grunting on their part, means that the performers won because you paid for your ticket in cash and the theater has a no-refund policy.

Do not fold your program into a close approximation of a B-52 and see if it will reach the orchestra pit. We know it's tempting but wait until your wife drags you to the Paris Opera where the draft is better for long flights.

Do not bring a snack in a paper bag to the ballet. Popcorn is not served at the theater, but there is a bar right outside the Dress Circle which, between programs, teems with other husbands who gratefully pay $7.00 for a small shot of scotch.

Do make comments during intermission like "I loved his early work but this slide back into Petipa is disturbing. Can *Sleeping Beauty* really be done again?" Or, "I've never seen something so sentimental from Balanchine before, this must have been created right after he immigrated. I detected at least six references to the Romantic period".

For the more advanced, a favorite way to pass the time during intermission is to choose a favorite choreographer or dancer (there are pictures of the dancers in the program). Then spend the season gushing about her growth as an artist, or complaining that she is not quite up to the complexities of the choreography tonight or pointing out that in the first program the steps were too complex and the dancers didn't have a chance to develop her own interpretation of the piece.

A very cool thing to do is to develop a distaste for a particular choreographer so you can criticize the efforts of the disliked artist with obscure and obfuscating terms gleaned from the program notes. Something along the lines of, "I don't know what possessed him to emulate Anthony Tudors' work in this new piece."

A quick Miss Behaved Guide to Dance Styles:

Classical dance is done in toe shoes (yes it hurts) and the dancers wear their hair up secured by tiara and/or feathers depending on whether they are princesses or birds. Classical ballerinas also wear those stiff-skirted sparkly tutus that entrance girls from ages 3 to 120 years.

Postclassical with a Russian twist is where you'll get into trouble every time. Just nod and look intelligent since there is often no plot except for the times when there is a plot. Often beautiful peasant girls go mad. Refer back to the laboriously written program notes. Remember this Miss Behaved rule: the longer the notes, the harder the ballet will be to understand.

Modern dance is performed barefoot. The dancers wear tie-dyed unitards and are allowed to toss their hair around a great deal. The dances will be choreographed by names like Val Caniparoli or Paul Taylor. If the dancers in the company resemble actual people (in that they have more than a single flat dimension to their bodies), you're watching the Bill T Jones Company. If the dancers are crawling all over each other and suspending themselves from places you'd get in trouble for suggesting at home, that company is Pilobolus. There is hardly any lifting or throwing in a Twyla Tharp piece. If you're enjoying yourself at all, you're watching Jerome Robbins or Agnes deMille (that's because they choreographed for the musical theater).

If men are dancing in toe shoes and wearing sparkly tutus in size 18, you've wandered into Les Ballets Trockadero de Monte Carlo, a Miss Behaved Company that turns famous ballets into parodies (think molting swans). Good for you, because your dance experience will actually be enjoyable.

Important survival tip

If you are ever faced with program notes that include explanations like, "An intimate solo in which the viewer has the feeling that he is looking into the soul of a man… Small isolated movements of the head, fingers, shoulders and even back muscles tell a tale of disappointment, (and) desire…and flailing arms of power and despair," you are doomed. It is best to duck the flailing arms of power and despair and grab a scotch from the bar on the way out. Your wife will eventually thank you, but don't push your luck and take her to the last hour of Wrestle Mania just because it too is in town.

Another quick way to determine if the dancing is modern or not is the music. Modern dance is often accompanied by music by composers like John Cage or Philip Glass and their music often sounds like banging and groaning pipes. One Miss Behaved husband started to go backstage calling out "Don't worry, I'm a professional plumber. I'll fix that rattle in no time."

This Miss Behaved guide is obviously good for only one emergency evening. It shouldn't be construed as a comprehensive guide that would get a person through a whole season, especially if there are 'new works' or 'new talent'. Because there is no possible way to predict if the piece will be noteworthy, we can't anticipate what a reluctant husband should say.

It's too bad a husband in your situation, faced with such danger, can't just hire a Stunt.

Dear Miss Behaved,

Is it Miss Behaved to shop for a swimsuit while surreptitiously munching on a bag of Mrs. Field's chocolate chip cookies hidden in my purse?

Signed,

Finding My Inner Miss Behaved Soul

Dear Satisfied,

Of course it's Miss Behaved.

Often the only thing that fits perfectly in the dressing room is the cookie in your hand.

Miss Behaved Fashion Moments

◆

Last season, women everywhere rejected the tyranny of pantyhose and wore their own bare legs under suits, dresses, and slacks. For a brief shining moment, this was heralded as not merely a trend, but a new way of dressing. According to *Vogue*, the barelegged look started well before spring, with young things wearing boots, wool scarves, and blue goosepimpled knees. The look was here to stay, claimed the fashion magazines.

On its natural surface, this seems a wonderfully Miss Behaved rejection of the old ways. Released from the twisted-legs, sagging at-the-crotch, bunching-at-the-ankle, hose requirement, women were finally liberated. We were free from snags, runs, and the eternal questions of nude, partial nude, suntan, black, clay, off-black, light black or midnight. We were no longer reminded that 'Queen' is not a compliment. With this new trend, women marched down the street—skirts swinging against bare calves, pumps digging into the backs of our bare heels—and we felt liberated. And we needed to purchase underwear.

In order to follow along with this new bare look, women had to spend proportionally more cash on better underwear. Underwear needed to be slippery so the panty-line didn't show under skirts. Underwear needed to be invisible under tight-cropped pants. Underwear needed to be nude, taupe, forest, lemon, dark cinnamon, lizard, or leopard skin. Trips to Victoria Secret had to be made.

Thongs are considered the most Miss Behaved design for underwear. They look fabulous on the showgirls in Vegas and they look impressive at the gym, where those women who give up comfort for style truly stand out. And of course, politically, the thong still carries references that even staunchly bipartisan Miss Behaved voters don't like to think about. (Republicans don't wear them at all). But for a smooth look under slacks and an afternoon of constant irritation, the thong is by far the best Miss Behaved option. Tiger stripe patterns are good; wear them with white cotton capris.

If the look for legs is bare, then the look for toes is manicured. Some Miss Behaved women, who had never once paid attention to their toenails but concentrated instead on world peace, found themselves at the salon trying to choose between passion plum or maniacal mulberry. With this new, casual, trend, women found themselves nurturing yet another 'neglected' body part. The new trend required buffed and painted toes that screamed, "I have time, money, the inclination to follow fads, and, yes, have painted my toe nails to display in these open-toed shoes, but I am not trying too hard."

Most Miss Behaved women admit that their political agenda encompasses everything but hairy legs, especially in the summer. However, winter was considered a reprieve especially during the happy cabled-tights phase. This new bare trend forced women into yet another evening ritual, an extra fixed agenda item in the morning or another trip to the drug store for hair removal products. Most women just shave in the shower, an activity that has the extra benefit of being dangerous. As you precariously balance in the tile shower stall one foot resting on the slippery floor, and the other suspended in mid-air, don't forget to inspect your toenails for chips in the polish.

Miss Behaved women know that white makes you look fat, dark colors make you look thin. No matter what those punky little models on the runway are doing to their own appendages, any women over the age of 25 will want a little color on her bare legs. There are options for color.

One can get a tan, which according to any pundit worth his breath is a terribly Miss Behaved thing to do because tanning has been categorized as a life-threatening activity. (Those same pundits don't wear skirts we hasten to add.) Or one can use a bottle of self-tanning lotion as long as one remembers to exfoliate first, reapply every five days, and be careful of streaking. (Don't get too much build up around the painted toe nails.) Or one can use a very expensive bottle of self-tanning lotion that doesn't streak but fades completely in just three days. (The price of the designer self-tanning lotion is equal to the price of two pairs of Donna Karan pantyhose purchased that one time during a crisis at an out–of–town convention.) So there is a little color, a lot of color, no color. In the old days it was just about nude pantyhose—in retrospect, a simpler option with no streaking.

For years the best-kept secret of Miss Behaved women was that control-top pantyhose, any kind of control-top pantyhose, smoothed, firmed, held in a stomach that had seen too many years of use, and, as a bonus, controlled that roiling butt.

Who has not stood in the dressing room of Macy's and assured her reflection that the bumps and rolls visible under the perfect on-sale skirt, would smooth out with the small addition of a pair of hose? Who has not depended on the spandex material in the panty part of the hose to create the illusion that the holiday season did no damage?

Take away our control-top pantyhose and suddenly we were responsible for calming that roiling butt all by ourselves. With no pantyhose option, Miss Behaved women all over the country were forced to join gyms, do endless crunches and try to quickly tone their inner thighs. This takes time, energy, and complete disregard for the reality that there will be no results until summer is over and wool slacks are back. Not to mention the trauma of competing with all that stylish underwear in the locker room.

The barelegged look was the ideal Miss Behaved fashion moment. Rejecting pantyhose had all the appearance of being fun, easy, and more comfortable, when it was actually far more work than any human woman had time for. Bare legs look casual and carefree, yet they must look perfect thus necessitating an increase in expensive products and services to maintain that look.

There is nothing better than a fashion trend that requires a great deal of internal work, effort, and cash in order to give the external impression that it is all quite easy.

The Miss Behaved advice:

Way back in March we suggested that you not throw out that good $30 pair of off-off dark-storm pantyhose just yet. And we were right. Not only that, the item to have this season is patterned leopard print-tights touted to be the best 'update' to the old tired wardrobe. And Miss Behaved women know how long that's likely to last.

Dear Miss Behaved,

Many sincere sales people have advised me that the right swimsuit size for me is a size larger than my dress size. I worked very hard to be the dress size I am. It's depressing to have to jump up a size in the swimsuit department and it's not even my fault. In fact, I don't like buying swimsuits for that reason. Doesn't this sound as if the swimsuit manufacturers are being Miss Behaved?

Signed,

Wrong Parts Squeezed Together

Dear Squeezed,

No, the swimsuit manufacturers are just being short-sighted, if not short-waisted. If the swimsuit industry were interested in actually selling more than one swimsuit per woman, per painful season, swimsuits would be manufactured to be two sizes larger than your dress size. In other words, if a woman wears a size 12 dress, then she would require a swimsuit in a size 8. Most Miss Behaved shoppers would buy many suits of that size and wear them inside out to show off the label.

With this new system, a woman would look forward to purchasing swimsuits since, no matter what she acquired during the holidays and a long cozy winter with big helpings of everything, her new swimsuit would have only increased by one size. She'd still be just a size 10 which is far less than the size 14 dress she had to purchase for the office party. She would buy three size 10 swimsuits just to prove she hadn't gained too much weight.

Miss Behaved pundits are surprised that no one in the swimsuit industry has conducted any marketing surveys or studies to discover this fact. What would it take to make this prediction? "In the future I see larger size swimsuits being sold to the fifty percent of the swimsuit buying population that is overweight according to one chart or another."

Certainly there should be at least one swimsuit company that could figure this out, create the suits, and make a killing.

Unless this represents a larger Miss Behaved conspiracy having to do with the supply of spandex and misogyny.

Country Pure Makeup

◆

Miss Behaved beauty-supply shoppers love the free-gift-with-purchase concept. For as little as $31.96 a Miss Behaved shopper can purchase a small lipstick and lip liner that qualifies her for a fabulous gift-with-purchase. The gift box usually contains one tiny vial of the latest magic elixir that will rejuvenate skin, another tiny bottle of lotion of which the Miss Behaved shopper already owns seven, two miniature lipsticks in brown, and a plastic comb. It doesn't matter if it's useful; it's free, packaged well, and brings Miss Behaved customers back on a predictable quarterly basis.

With the holidays in the air, and free promotional bags on the department store shelves, a Miss Behaved friend reports that this season's free gift is definitely worth the hour she stood in line. Her gift included, among other useful things, a plastic mirror and a sample of the new fructose/lactose eye cream to reduce the appearance of fine lines. (Miss Behaved women know that to permanently reduce the appearance of deep lines a girl needs a shot of botox.)

But while gloating over her gift-with-purchase packaged in a plastic yet colorful and eye-catching pink-and-yellow bag, this Miss Behaved shopper was momentarily distracted by something even more new and novel. Just to the left of those mysterious and far too dark eye shadows by Chanel, a new cosmetic counter gleamed like a beacon in the night. Or it could have been the spotlights trained onto the counter from overhead.

The new cosmetic line was called the Country Remedy Solution. Straw was strewn on the floor in front of the counter; girls dressed in overalls clustered around the shelves like flies on honey. One fresh-faced young thing spied our Miss Behaved shopper and hollered a friendly hello and how are you?

"How's your mother with that bursitis thing?" The girl bellowed. "And how's your brother's drinking problem?"

Curious as to how the girl knew about the brother who was planning to announce his problem over a bottle of good Merlot during Thanksgiving dinner, our Miss Behaved friend quickly approached the counter if only to quiet the enthusiastic greeting.

"Hi," the girl said again. "Welcome to the Country. We're just down home here with the all-natural solutions for the busy woman." She squinted at our friend and her freckled nose wrinkled. "You are a busy woman, aren't you?"

Our friend nodded absently, thinking that if that brother did announce his problem, would that upstage her youngest sister who planned to come out? And just to be safe, should she put away the Baccarat and serve the wine in paper cups? Was there a Martha Stewart book on how to fold paper cups in such a fashion so that they gave the appearance of Baccarat crystal?

But she was quickly distracted from dinner seating arrangements by the enchanting rows of small, medium, and large jars covered with gingham material, tied with raffia, and lined up along the counter like jam jars at the county fair. The sales girl, her wood-burned nametag read *Ellie*, hauled up a picnic basket filled with samples.

"We're just down home here," Ellie explained. "We have the beauty treatments you always knew were good for you but never used because they weren't packaged into cute little containers. Here, try this." She cut open a lemon and shoved our friend's elbow into one half.

"Now, this is our newest product, the egg mask." Ellie opened a colorful egg carton decorated with the gingham and bows. "This here is a package of a half dozen eggs good for two weeks. The instructions are inside. You only need to use one egg per application, see how they're self-contained? Makes them easier to use. Course you have to keep this refrigerated at all times. And it won't last, so you'll have to come back all the time for refills."

"Perfect." Murmured our friend.

Ellie's next item appeared to be a beer bottle. "Rinse for your hair to make it shiny, we have a sale on this for only $14.75. Oh sure, you can pay less in the grocery store, but there wouldn't be instructions and waivers and this cute bow that matches your egg carton."

Our friend asked how Ellie achieved her fresh healthy glow.

"Well if you city girls got outside once in a while...."

Ellie was cut off by a matronly woman in a classic house dress, by Simplicity. "We don't advocate too much sun of course. Here in the Country, we are very conscious of skin care."

"Oh, you have a cream? Something with oxygen?" Our friend looked around and noticed a sign that advertised a "Full Shade System." Guaranteed to keep skin young and fresh as a country spring breeze.

"No creams or gimmicks here in the Country," the matronly saleswoman explained patiently. "Our shade system is easy and guaranteed, but you must use it all the time." The matron pulled out a poke bonnet, straight out of the costume department for *Little House on the Prairie*. An effective system, yes; practical when backing the car out of the parking lot, no.

"Do you do animal testing?" Our conscientious friend inquired.

"Well," replied Ellie, "we tried to get Clyde, that's my favorite pig, to wear some of our berry juice blush for a day? But he wouldn't hold still and ate half the product."

She pulled out a beautiful jar of purple berry jam and handed it over. "Berry stain. Works great, won't rub off during the day. It's $65, but it will last you. No sugar"

"Makes a great cobbler." Chimed in the manager. "You can use it for a lip stain as well. We have smaller jars than that to carry in your basket."

"Do you have anything for de-stressing the skin?"

"Oh sure, we have our mud mask, it's from what was left of our top-soil on the farm. We canned it and brought it here. You know there are a bunch of fancy places in California where people spend $100 bucks to sit in mud. Heck I can join Clyde for free anytime I want."

"You mean Calistoga."

"Yup, and it's right here." She pulled out a Mason jar of dark stuff, hopefully not from Clyde's private collection. "And," Ellie continued, "you can use it right now. You don't even have to drive nowhere. Cause we know how busy you gals are."

The choices were varied and many. Our Miss Behaved shopper discussed the benefits of the mud, fresh avocado either whole or mashed, milk bath, and what looked like sand.

She held up the sand.

"Well you know how taking dead flakes off is a really big deal for looking younger?" Ellie explained. "You know, you can just scrub some sand on your face and get the same effect. Our sand is competitively priced at $15 a tube, and it's only that much because it's so hard to get the sand into these little packages."

Our Miss Behaved shopper picked up a package of hand cream—thick, natural, with a texture that felt suspiciously like lard—but where else could she find that? And she took a jar of the mud.

Ellie happily took the store credit card and wrapped the purchases in a scrap of material tied at the top with string.

As she returned our friend's credit card, Ellie leaned over and whispered, "I'll tell you something. You want to look younger and prettier?"

Our friend nodded, clutching her favorite gift-with-purchase package that included this new chin-firming cream sample that will reduce the appearance of sagging skin.

"Sit on your porch in the afternoon and say hey to the neighbors."

"Sit down?" Our friend tired to calculate the last time she sat down at home. She drew a complete blank.

"Try it," encouraged Ellie. "After a month, you won't even need our stuff."

Dear Miss Behaved,

We are right in the middle of planning my wedding. Only 11 months to go! It's practically here! We have edited the guest list down to 500 names on my side, 30 on the groom's. Thirteen of my closest friends, including a woman I used to nod hello to in the library, have already ordered their custom made bridesmaid dresses and shoes.

My bridesmaids say that mustard yellow satin is something that can't be worn again, but I assured them that is not the case, and isn't the cost of the bridesmaid dress equal to the number of guests invited? On the bride's side? I think that's the formula, but that's not why I'm writing.

My problem is that my father is not getting into the sprit of the wedding at all. Just the other day I overheard him begging my fiancée to take the half million dollars and invest in a house. He even offered to throw in the old Mercedes if we agreed to elope. Is Dad losing it?

Signed,

Overwrought and Overbought

Dear Should Be Over It,

No, your father is not losing it, he is merely suffering from the Miss Behaved malady Pre-nuptial Stress Syndrome. This syndrome usually first manifests in the father of the bride and quickly spreads to the father of the groom, the mother of the groom, and various relatives who have attended one too many Miss Behaved shower luncheons. There is no cure per se, unless you agree to elope and invest in real estate instead of investing in the cake decorations that look like perfect lilies at only $25 per flower. (Always ask for blue since the food coloring will stain the guest's teeth, great for just before the family photos).

By the actual day of the wedding, the only person not affected with Pre-nuptial Stress syndrome is the bride.

Typical Miss Behaved brides are not, under any circumstances, and certainly not to alleviate the terminal symptoms of stress suffered by family, willing to forgo being the center of attention during the event of the decade. Because of this expected attitude, their family is only allowed temporary relief from Pre-nuptial Stress. This usually takes the form of nasty comments about either the bride's weight or the groom's career prospects and dubious past.

But you are asking for some Miss Behaved advice.

It's far too early in the planning stages to elope. Miss Behaved brides never elope until after the nonrefundable down payment has been made to the caterer, the invitations mailed, the brides maids custom dresses paid in full, and cost of your gown is charged to your mother's American Express card (no limit). Only then can the Miss Behaved bride discover that it's all so meaningless and ditch the whole thing.

If you can't schedule in an elopement, you can always cancel the wedding. This has the advantage of calling even more attention to you for an even longer period of time. People will talk about you for years to come. But don't do it until the cake and most of the gifts have arrived.

Since neither option seems viable for you, simply ignore your father and take your fiancée to the bridal boutiques where many a bride spends happy hours comparing the dresses at the boutique with her own superior one and her fiancée quickly learns not to express his opinion, good practice for a Miss Behaved marriage.

The Eighth Grade Dress Code

◆

Dear Miss Behaved,

I just went to my son's eighth grade graduation and was shocked at the outfits these girls were allowed to wear. They were all dressed like prostitutes! My son was so dumbfounded he could barely wrest his eyes from the spectacle. Are these girls being Miss Behaved?

Signed,

Simply Shocked in the Third Row

Dear Simply,

You did not say so, but you are correct in labeling those eighth-grade girls as Miss Behaved. These girls were Miss Behaved not because they wore a thin cotton shift, $40 at Old Navy, with large chunky shoes and bare legs in public. They are Miss Behaved because they CAN wear a thin cotton shift, $40 at Old Navy, with large chunky shoes and bare legs in public. Who better to wear short, thin, dresses than girls with skinny, undeveloped, thighs that don't rub together when they walk?

Most Miss Behaved people agree that it would be far more shocking to see a woman who is deeply involved in sensible middle age dressed the same way. Unless of course, she's a trophy wife. Then we can pass around gossip far more salacious than the fact that she dresses like an eighth-grader.

Many sincere people would love to dress the younger generation in appropriate clothing. The challenge is that appropriate has been replaced with the Miss Behaved notion that a girl can wear what she wants. And really, if short, flimsy, dresses are not worn by young girls, by default it would mean those dresses must be worn by the mothers of young girls. Because someone is shopping at Old Navy.

To allay the immediate fear that grown women are wearing half grown shifts, a quick Miss Behaved survey determined that very few women with children old enough to be the center of attention at a typical middle-school graduation ceremony were prepared to leave the house wearing nothing more than a layer of cheap cotton and string bikini underwear.

Which leaves us with the fearless girls. But please, don't let graduation be the last time your sensibilities are assaulted, save energy for the really Miss Behaved event, the prom.

Every May, protests and eyebrows are raised over the chosen attire of young things attending the biggest night of their lives. There are Miss Behaved comments to be made about the Prom in general but, for this argument, let's stick to the dress. Every year the girls shop for the perfect dress and every year otherwise sensible parents abdicate control, feeling that if there is going to be a fight, there are larger battles to win than what the kid will wear for one night. And without fail there is protest about the chosen prom ensembles by one group or another the members of which either didn't dress at all when they were seventeen or their only entrée to the prom was to volunteer for clean up. In small towns this issue often makes the lifestyle section of the local paper.

The Miss Behaved opinion is that there is no group better equipped to wear some slinky, backless, middle less, strapless, spandex, prom dress than 17-year-old girls who can hold up and hold in every single inch of their parts all by themselves without medical or technical aid.

Many Miss Behaved women feel that someone should enjoy wearing those tankinis. Someone needs to purchase those huge clunky shoes that were marked down almost immediately because the women with money wouldn't think of wearing something so ridiculous. Someone beside pop stars should be willing and able to wear the dictates of fashion. It's a dirty job; it's best to leave it to the young.

The real Miss Behaved question is: should we whisper to these young things that this wonderful window of opportunity only stays open for about two years? Less if they spend their freshman year in college ordering pizza with extra cheese every other night? Should we give them 'The Talk' about cellulite? Share with them that what lies ahead is a lifelong battle devoted to keeping what they have right now?

They will look like you soon enough. You can always take your son to a real prostitute so he can compare.

The Definitive Wedding Guide for Confused Brides

◆

Dear Miss Behaved,

I'm getting married in two years, we have the reception site reserved, the dress will be shipped from France and flowers ordered. I only need a groom, but two years is plenty of time for that. Do you have some advice concerning the rest of the details?

Signed,

Obviously Not Enough *Bride's Magazine* in the House.

Dear Always the Bride,

Since everyone has wedding advice, it behooves us to add in our own Miss Behaved vision for the perfect Miss Behaved wedding:

Cocktail Napkins

Always make sure the cocktail napkins match the complimentary matchbooks.

Miss Behaved guests are very sensitive and in order for them to enjoy themselves at your wedding, all the correct wedding items should be in evidence:

Monogrammed napkins.

Matchbook covers decorated with cameo portraits of the groom and bride.

Interlocking champagne glasses, so useful for that single toast of a life time and so perfect for catching dust on the mantel afterwards.

A cake knife with a large bouquet attached to the handle that is so large the bride must use two hands to steady it and the size inspires the groom to make a tasteless comment about the main prop for *Halloween*.
Colored beer to match the napkins.

Why is all this attention to detail necessary? Miss Behaved guests, as well as the bride, know that the color and font size on the cocktail napkins have a direct correlation to the future success of the marriage itself. A poor napkin-color choice is often the first in a long line of unintended mistakes that lead to years of unhappiness. And there will be additional recriminations during the first anniversary when the young couple discovers that the only napkins they can afford are the leftover ones from the reception, and they don't match the china.

Most Miss Behaved couples will spend the appropriate amount of time debating the pros and cons of each variation of napkin. A Miss Behaved amount of time would be about seven months. Matchbook covers should take a little less time, about five months, but only if the Miss Behaved bride remembers to bring up the subject every day.

Wedding Invitations

Miss Behaved wedding invitations should be as expressive as the Miss Behaved love the couple feels for one another. For instance, an invitation we recently received was written on an oversized card decorated with real lace and three-dimensional hearts that jumped for joy when the invitation was opened. It frightened the cat.

Another Miss Behaved wedding invitation sported a photomontage of the bride and groom as children. On the inside the only information listed was the URL to the couple's web site. She reluctantly logged on because the guest in this case was a relative. The couple's site not only displayed the time and place of the wedding (where the guests were invited to share in the perfect union of two individual beings who want to walk together in a separate but totally equal way), it also included fifty additional pages with pastel backgrounds explaining in detail every moment of the couple's engagement. Pages included a webcam trained on the wedding dress hanging in the guestroom and video of the proposal. The cocktail-napkin link alone was five pages.

Another Miss Behaved invitation played the theme to *Titanic* when it was opened. One friend couldn't get the music to stop and was forced to immerse the entire invitation in the swimming pool, which meant she lost the particulars on the location of the reception as well as a quick outline of what the couple wanted as gifts. She isn't sorry.

Most Miss Behaved invitations are stuffed with confetti that floats around the guest's house for days adhering to all surfaces (or clogging the pool filter).

Miss Behaved invitations never include reply cards with stamps.

Music
Accordions are an excellent Miss Behaved highlight to any wedding reception, especially if a polka band is unavailable or if the remaining members of the Grateful Dead aren't up for it. Miss Behaved accordion song choices include *RawHide*, *I Want Your Sex*, and any other song guaranteed to insult and dismay. Remember this is a family event.

Timing
When setting the wedding date, it is important to interrupt other people's lives as thoroughly and in the most inconvenient way as possible so they will always remember your wedding day.

For instance, hold the wedding on the Saturday of Thanksgiving break. This date has the advantage of not only using up a perfectly good Saturday in a boring and unnecessary way, but by holding the ceremony and reception slap dab in the middle of a four-day weekend, the Miss Behaved bride can command attention for all of that weekend. Guests cannot go anywhere or make any other plans except to stay home and attend her wedding. Labor Day weekend or Memorial Day weekend would also be good Miss Behaved wedding dates.

Place

Out-of-town is always a popular Miss Behaved wedding destination. Hold your wedding on a beach in the Cayman Islands. This is perfect because it's expensive, difficult to reach, and you can claim that it will be just a simple ceremony on the beach. Make guests wear black tie.

Babies

Of course the Miss Behaved bride should bring the baby to the wedding, but only if she's marrying the father. Otherwise the baby should just attend the reception.

Wedding Shower

A surprise wedding shower is the perfect venue in which the soon-to-be sisters-in-law can demonstrate their Miss Behaved affection for the suprisee (sometimes referred as the bride).

The most important element in a surprise shower is to arrange for the guest of honor to show up to the surprise party clad in what she normally wears to change the oil in the car. If she is also having a bad hair day, so much the better.

A Miss Behaved surprise shower guest list should always include a handful of resentful relatives who are prone to gossip and whom the bride-to-be has already tried to impress during Thanksgiving dinner. According to them, unsuccessfully.

Take as many pictures of the astonished bride upon her arrival as possible. Take more as she unwraps completely inappropriate and useless gifts like scratchy lingerie, ten-gallon silver coffee urns, and dish towels in brown plaid and appliquéd kittens. Don't forget to take a number of photographs of the makeup-less bride-to-be next to her elaborately coifed sisters-in-law and aunts so the givers of the party can later reminisce, "We looked so much better than her."

It is important to note that, for the most part, the givers of Miss Behaved surprise showers are the same women who just shelled out $350 for an infamous Miss Behaved bridesmaid dress. Sometimes a surprise shower for the bride who chose those dresses is the only appropriate Miss Behaved response.

But remember you need to play games. We recommend the popular "guess the bride's weight."

Dear Miss Behaved,

What happened to my favorite part of Christmas, the family letter? There is nothing more thrilling than to learn the second ex-wife of my best friend's ex-husband held a family reunion at Sturgis, South Dakota. I miss learning that kind of valuable information. When did those letters die out?

Signed,

Nothing to Read during the Holidays

Dear Nothing,

The letters didn't die, they evolved. We have abandoned the once favored practice of writing impossibly cheerful letters with only slightly exaggerated family news to our friends, and even more exaggerated news to the extended family and replaced them with web sites of enormous proportions and narcissism.

It is a practice that can only be admired by the truly Miss Behaved, and we do.

So in the Family Christmas Letter Contest, the ultimate Miss Behaved Christmas letter is now nothing more than a tiny business card sent in the big envelope with the two lines we now love to read: Merry Christmas, visit our web site at www.geocities.com/family/smith/Nancy& Tony_145/. So we did.

On the site we found 14 pictures of Tony Jr. in his various little league poses. A film clip of the birth of baby number four. Audio of the school play where Misty wasn't the star but held an important supporting part that required memorizing 17 lines, not counting the gasps and nods that she did so well (Click here for video clips of the three parts where she speaks). A rotating graphic of how the family finances have increased this year because of Tony's new job in telecommunications, a very hot industry.

Click here to see the current stock prices of Nancy's company.

Fill out the following questions and compare your income against ours to see how you stack up.

Click here to see how we're spending the inheritance Nancy's family just left us. We're considering a BMW Z-3 and jet skis, or a RV and a Jeep. Log in and tell us which would be best.

Click here to read from Nancy's current novel in progress. Remember it's still a draft, so when you fill out the enclosed evaluation and order form, be kind.

Here's a video clip of the family serving soup at the local homeless shelter in honor of Flag Day. Click here for testimonials. We were there for a whole hour, except for Tony who had to leave after ten minutes for a meeting back at work.

The main site linked to the children's own sites. Tony Jr's site played four minutes of Britney Spears from video clips he's borrowed off of other sites. Misty's site was composed entirely of a collage of In Sync, Back Street Boys, and 98 degrees, all of whom, to the untrained eye, look alike.

There was a picture of the family standing in line for *Star Wars* captioned with "Doesn't Tony Jr. look cute as Bobba Fet? Misty wanted to dress up as Queen Amidala but we couldn't get the hair right. We were the first family in our neighbor hood to see the new blockbuster movie."

At the bottom of the web page was an invitation to communicate. "If you have anything to say that matches up with our superb technological lives, you can e-mail the webmaster, who is Todd, our ten-year-old. Or call on any number of our cell phones, see numbers listed below."

Anyone who has ever wandered onto the Yahoo web site devoted to the adventures of Sammy the Sloth, feels immediately compelled to not only improve, but to create their own site for fun and possibly profit. Miss Behaved people understand. But be warned that merely creating a web site will not count towards your fifteen minutes of fame, and it doesn't count as information we need.

What a Miss Behaved web site visitor and newsletter recipient really wants to know is how do you feel about me?

Discovering Miss Behaved Roots

◆

Dear Miss Behaved,

All my friends are now involved in looking for the highest branches in their family tree while simultaneously feeling a deep connection with their roots. I also hear that discovering new family members is an excellent excuse to purchase expensive genealogy computer programs and take trips to Salt Lake City. I am also interested in spending months ignoring the children in order to focus on elaborate Internet searches for family members who are, to the best of my knowledge, dead.

But I'm worried that rather than being Miss Behaved, genealogy is just popular.

Signed,

Worried Because I Don't Have Much of a Past

Dear Past,

One of the biggest benefits of uncovering family history is to discover salient facts that will aid you in pinpointing family tendencies that will help exonerate you from self-improvement efforts. (For example if laziness runs in the family, what is a person to do?) Plus genealogical charts are a big help when you make your argument for why you are the most deserving of all the second cousins twice-removed on Aunt Fortuna's side to inherit everything from cousin

Lloyd who you heard has buried a fortune in gold coins in his basement. Both those activities are Miss Behaved.

Working day and night to collect names to decorate the sprouting branches of the family tree because you believe your own children will be fascinated with your findings is just misguided.

Those good reasons aside, there is a Miss Behaved approach to connecting with your roots: keep them shallow. We are Miss Behaved enough to believe that even Genealogy should be more about stories and less about amassing family names as if they were a collection of glass birds. To this end, we share this report from a Miss Behaved researcher who recently discovered the traditions and history of the native homeland her mother rejected over forty years ago.

As I age, I long for more connections to the heritage and traditions of the old country my mother left behind. I want a definitive explanation for my fatalism, snap judgements, and obsessing about situations over which I have no control. I want to be able to point to all my problems, then point to corresponding family members and assign blame.

My mother immigrated when she was only 18 with little more than a trunk full of linen suits and admission to the University. Once there, she met and married a native and they located to a small town in the Gold Country that was not only rich in the history and lore of her newly adopted home, but featured in *Sunset Magazine* on a quarterly basis.

I remember that like most first-generation immigrants, my mother refused to replicate the old ways in the new land. She encouraged us to speak the adoptive country's language and embrace the local habits that made life in the new environment easier. For instance, contrary to her upbringing, it was not necessary to purchase a new spring coat because spring was warm. It was not necessary to wear snowsuits because it only snowed one month a year. It was not necessary to wear fur; you'd just get paint on it.

We did, of course visit my mother's family for a few weeks to pacify the grandparents. They rarely considered even a month-long visit enough time. I remember my grandmother's predictable greeting as soon as the family walked into her house. "Well, you're just going to leave in a month."

My mother dressed in shorts; my grandmother dressed in pantyhose, girdles, full slips, and dresses with belts. She wore high-heel shoes. Even for hikes. I later wondered about the logic of burning tons of fossil fuel to cool entire buildings in order to maintain that post-war dress code, but by then I had internalized at least one Old World rules; keep my opinions to myself.

When we visited the homeland, the most important social event of the week was Sunday Brunch at the Club. Every week my grandmother's people sat still for two hours and consumed large slabs of meat the likes of which could only be seen in specialty restaurants in our own native land. We could only look on with wonder and awe.

We were very fortunate as children. My grandmother's friends were quite liberal and tried not to blame us for our mixed heritage. (They worried we would contract AIDS by living so close to San Francisco, three hours away.) They patted us on the head, offered us a sip of their martini and heaped five tablespoons of Thousand Island dressing over our single wedge of iceberg lettuce.

As we matured, keeping quiet became a critical feature of our visits to the homeland. We were not allowed to mention some of the stranger customs in our own country—the fresh fruit in December, the bare feet in February, the favorite uncles who shared the same bed when they visited our beach house. We were not allowed to correct the prevailing belief in the homeland that wine drinkers were winos while decent people who ordered three scotch and waters in a row were just thirsty.

My wonderful grandmother declared once that she would never allow a Democrat to sit at her dinner table. We did not point out that her stance would require that every member of the second and third generation of the family (all emigrated from the homeland to other parts of the country) would have to eat outside.

The Western part of my background used to be my primary way of identifying myself, particularly when traveling in Europe. But now claiming heritage from this new part of the world is in vogue, which is the whole point of bringing it up in the first place. There are more television shows set in the homeland; there is more acceptance and tolerance for the ways of the people of the homeland. As Americans wallow in over-exposure and talk shows, there is a growing belief that perhaps a little Lutheran sternness and silence is not such a bad idea after all.

But I don't bring that up over the weekly tofu-riddled confessional dinners with my Democrat friends.

So after many, many years of denial (a way of life in my mother's land) and months of listening to *Prairie Home Companion*, I can finally admit that, yes, my people are pale, eat hot dishes, and consider worrying a contact sport.

I am Midwestern on my mother's side.

However, since the release of the film *Fargo*, my mother admits to nothing.

On the Job, the Miss Behaved E-Mail Retrieval Unit Findings

◆

The idea that the principals in a company can and should retrieve, read, and ponder any old e-mail message sent to and from their old, current, and new employees is very Miss Behaved. To have that much time on one's hands is a Miss Behaved sign of a complete lack of productive projects and focus and should be commended.

There was the case of Microsoft's incriminating e-mails discussing how to take over the world, and it still stands as one of the better excuses to burrow around other people's hard drives. But it's pretty clear that there are few companies like Microsoft and hardly any companies filled with employees who have enough corps de esprit to launch a nefarious plot together, let alone get someone else to volunteer to write it all down and share with the rest of the group.

None the less, intrepid Miss Behaved investigators dove into the dark cyberspace of Paranoid Company B in their vigorous attempt to unearth subversive activities and get mentioned in the next *Newsweek* article on corporate crime. The goal? To plumb a mystery that has baffled modern companies since WWII: why does the sink in the break room reproduce dirty coffee cups?

Suspicious e-mails written by Miss Behaved employees

Has anyone seen my stapler, it's my favorite one, the one that can punch through my 36 page reports. It has two hello kitty stickers on the top, please return. No questions asked.

Donuts in the break room Happy Friday!

Note from HR: Who left the coffee maker on over the weekend! We've been over this before; we're lucky a fire wasn't started! Remember the last person to leave the building needs to check all electrical equipment!

The copy machine e is down again remember you guys, use tray three only and if you need to use the letterhead and remember to put it in upside with the top facing away from you as you stand to the left of the machine or facing you as you stand to the right of the machine. Letterhead put in the top tray needs to be loaded upside down; letterhead put in the second tray needs to be loaded right side up. The third tray is the only tray that will accept colored paper. Until the repairperson returns my calls hand feed all labels.

Going away party for Tom; 4:50 in the break room, there are still a few donuts left

Advertising staff, meeting in five minutes, we're now in the small conference room because another group took over the big conference room at the last minute without reserving it or asking anyone. We have a sign up calendar at the front desk people, remember to use it!

Just a reminder, clean up your own dirty dishes, your mother doesn't live here.

Does anyone know how to repair a desk fountain? My meditation fountain seems to be broken and it's really stressing me out. Thanks ahead of time.

We noticed a disturbing trend of employees leaving the building at 4:55, please remember to stay and work diligently until 5:00, thank you.

It's my turn to clean out the refrigerator. I'm throwing everything away, if you have something you want to save or eat for lunch, get it now!

Who has my scissors? They're the black handled ones with really sharp blades. Two Xena stickers on the handle. Last seen in the copy room.

Does anyone have an annual report I can borrow?

Does anyone remember that during the last communication meeting the Mediator suggested that we all wash our own dishes? Using my "I" words, I'd like to say that I think we should wash all our own dishes, let's not let that productive five hour discussion go to waste!

Pam, can you get my diet Pepsi out of the refrigerator before someone throws it away? I have a meeting in the small conference room and can't get to the kitchen.

Who is using all the letter head?

That's a good thought Maryann, I suggest we bring this up at the next staff meeting, we all signed the agreement that we would take responsibility for the sink. If people are not honoring their commitment we may need to take some time and re-evaluate our mission statement.

Who left the lean cuisine chicken and pasta dinner in the freezer? It's been there since Sept.

Well, I'm leaving on vacation. We're off to Tahiti and then Bora Bora; boy those cut backs and lay offs sure paid off for the rest of us didn't they? Oh, sorry Tom.

I agree, she's not up to par at all, but we can't fire her because (message garbled)

It's not me, I don't even like chicken, ask Tiffany.

I'll be out at meetings all day, have a good weekend!

When is the next staff meeting? Is it every other Thursday or every other Tuesday?

I'm off to my brothers' wedding in Ohio. It will be a big family reunion. You can reach me at his house 808-966-3434 or on my cell phone 555-222-5534, or my pager 393-449-9958, my e-mail on the road is Yoyo@yahoo.com. Feel free to contact me at any time. Please.

I'm home with a sick kid, call me at home.

Bye all, it's been fun working with you but I'm really excited about an opportunity that came up just yesterday. See you in dot-com land!—Tom

It's every other Tuesday starting with the first Tuesday of the month unless the Tuesday falls after a major holiday, then the meeting is switched to the first Thursday of the month followed by the third Tuesday of the month. We had the last meeting on the first Thursday this month and now it will be the Third Tuesday, which was yesterday.

Has any one seen the Rogers report? It's missing from my credenza and I have a meeting in five minutes.

I think the chicken was Tom's

The report should be on Sue's desk, she had some last minute changes, check with her, you'll need twenty copies for the meeting. Remember not to use any letterhead and to stand to the right of the machine.

I think Tom will be back.

The Tragedy
of the Hopelessly Organized

◆

Dear Miss Behaved,

As I contemplate rewriting my club's bylaws because I'm the president for the third year in a row while waiting for another batch of brownies to be finished so I can wrap them for the PTA bake sale. And as I consider my strategy to update the company web site, I realize that the biggest compliment anyone has ever paid me was "you're so organized." My problem with this is I always wanted to be artistic. I want to be seen as creating projects that are beautiful and interesting. I want to hear; "You're so talented and clever." But I don't, I get; "You're so organized". Is this really a compliment? Can I be organized and also be Miss Behaved?

Signed,

Still in Pain Over Lost Opportunities I Couldn't Fit In

Dear in Pain, But It's a Well Defined and Easy to Locate Pain,

Miss Behaved people often give the compliment, "you're so organized", to people who are clearly not Miss Behaved. What the Miss Behaved person is really saying is, "Even though you not only follow all the prescribed systems inherit in society but put them in labeled, color-coded folders, we still think you're a nice person". Worse and even more Miss Behaved is the subtext of that compliment which is, "Well, you're unimaginative and a little bit boring, but at least you're organized. Can you help me find my keys?"

It's the Miss Behaved experience that very organized people, or at least people blamed for being organized, really want to be artistic. And artistic people don't care. So you're right. Miss Behaved people are always creative, hardly ever put their keys in the same place twice, and they don't care because being Miss Behaved is more fun than being organized and responsible.

But the organized person can become more Miss Behaved. We wouldn't leave a question like this dangling without a Miss Behaved answer.

Our advice is three pronged: hire an intervention team, join a support group, and finally we have some quick Miss Behaved tips to help shake you of your sensible habits.

The first Miss Behaved step that will take you quickly away from the organized dependable person you used to be, is the intervention step. Trained Miss Behaved professionals will evaluate your office and immediately remove the colored folders, labelers, index cards, staggered file holders, and the headset. They will leave behind nothing more than scraps of recycled paper on which you now must write important messages to just pile randomly on the desk. Once you've lost a couple of key accounts because of your inability to remember where you put the client's phone number, you'll discover not only that the world did not end, but that if you look pathetic enough, your coworkers, after a heavy collective sigh, will find your information for you. They will also take over the meeting you forgot about, and back you up when the last minute deadline overwhelms you and you need extra help. It always happens this way—the more competent cover for the disorganized. Remember how you used to help your coworkers on a daily basis? Now it's your turn. And with their help at every turn, now you have time for those long lunches you could never figure out how to squeeze in before.

Once your time is freed up because other people have taken over parts of your job, you can join a support group.

The Organized In Crisis Support Group is very tricky to find. You must call every day to find out where the meeting will be held because it never occurred to the people in charge to create a specific and consistent date and time for the meetings. They just get together when they feel like it and forget to call half the members when they finally decide. But it's okay; the members forgive, forget, and persevere.

Remember that this Miss Behaved Organized in Crisis Support Group never actually accomplishes anything, but they do enjoy eating the free cookies and drinking too much coffee. Members introduce themselves because the nametags were forgotten again, acknowledge that a higher power is involved in their lives (although no one can remember just exactly who that higher power is) and new members confess to tragic random moments of organization. Then all the members nod, offer encouragement to each other by calling out affirmations they read from the posters on the wall and they get home in time for *Ally McBeal.*

For our readers who still aren't certain they need help to leave their compulsively organized ways, we offer examples pulled from the minutes of the last known Miss Behaved Organized in Crisis meeting. These notes were scribbled with the stub of a lip pencil on the back of a crumpled flyer fished from the trash.

John admitted he once alphabetized all the cans in the kitchen cabinet, filed all the children's homework by class, and stacked the *Playboy* magazines by date for quick reference.

Susan confessed that she reads the catalogue for Franklin planners with the same intensity that most Miss Behaved readers reserve for *Cosmo* (or the July issue of *Playboy,* John can get Issue 91 for you). She admits she fantasizes about discovering an even more organized system than the one she already owns.

Steve disclosed that he attends *Get Organized* seminars just to keep up on the latest organized trends. He admits that he just loves being confirmed in his own sick need to file all the bank statements in a loose leaf binder so they are easy to read, and that he files all the money market fund statements into the correct folders.

One member confessed that she strongly believed that if she just turned the mattress on the schedule listed in the mattress instructions everything would be okay.

Many members confess to being hopelessly attached to the idea of file cabinets in the guestroom and always keeping a pencil and paper by the phone.

For those organized beings who still aren't certain that they had a problem at all, especially since their siblings are so grateful they remembered to send birthday cards to family members this year, we have a few notable danger signs.

Do you compulsively make lists and check them off even though two thirds of the items have already been finished for days, but you still like to write them down so you can make a 'finished' notation? Worse, are you so organized that you don't need to put the easy stuff like 'eat lunch' or 'get to work on time' on the list? Do you put real items of accomplishment like ' move the yard of gravel from the front of the house to the back', 'study for CBEST', or 'get advanced degree in time for next job review'?

Have you never, ever been overdrawn at the bank, always write down ATM with drawls, and have never needed to make only the minimum payment for the Visa and the MasterCard? Do you keep a running monthly budget and the target amounts per category taped to the inside of the checkbook cover? Do you pay attention to the list?

Do you not only remember to take your film in to be printed on a regular basis but remember to pick it up? Bonus points if you can open the packages of photos and identify every guest at your child's birthday party. Do you carefully place and label each photo into Volume 24 of the family photo albums?

Do you change the oil in the car every 3,000 miles?

Do you water the houseplants? Consistently? And if you don't water the plants is it because you set up a clever indoor drip system that takes care of the plants 24/7 and you just enjoy their green abundance?

If you are puzzled about any of the above questions, wondering why anyone would be so Miss Behaved as to mock the laudable and necessary virtues of being completely organized and in control of every second of every day, remember the above plea from Still in Pain Over Lost Opportunities I Couldn't Fit In.

No one cares that you are organized. In fact, the organized and responsible person just gets more work. Miss Behaved people know this and try to spend as much time as possible losing things, missing meetings, and forgetting deadlines so as not to be asked to do too much.

Most Miss Behaved people already know how to avoid contributing more than just bread and wine to the family Thanksgiving dinner, it's time to move on to the advanced class. If you don't want to be president of the PTA this year nor do you wish to plan the next family reunion, remember to practice the above suggestions. To become more Miss Behaved and less organized, just forget to pick up the children from school three days in a row, miss the next two PTA meetings, and lose the fundraising raffle tickets. This is not only very Miss Behaved, this irresponsible behavior has the added advantage of freeing up a great deal of your time so you can take that trip to the artist colony in New Mexico.

Remember to buy the plane tickets 21 days in advance.

Big Miss Behaved Women

◆

The average Miss Behaved woman is so confident, beautiful, and vibrant that the first impression upon meeting her is that she is thin.

Why thin? Because in this country, if a woman is beautiful she is thin. If she is beautiful and thin, then it follows that at some point in her socially acceptable career, she was a model, or she wanted to be a model, or that she could, at any time, step in front of a camera and be a model. In a visually oriented society to be beautiful is to be photographed.

But to be known and remembered, one has to do and be something, not just end up little more than a flattened image on a glossy page.

Miss Behaved women are lovely in a real-time passionate way. Miss Behaved women do not pose for pictures on a regular basis; they are not perpetually ready for their close-up. The current phenomena of living through the camera and videotaping life experiences for later viewing strikes many Miss Behaved people as a rather odd and detached way of living.

Consequently, the Miss Behaved family camera often holds a roll of film that begins with the children's first day of kindergarten and ends, 36 frames later, with junior high graduation. Many Miss Behaved parents are so busy watching the children that they forget to pick up the camera.

One of the more Miss Behaved life skills is to dispense with the camera completely. This frees the Miss Behaved woman to concentrate on real life, which, in most cases, is where we all live.

What kind of real life is the Miss Behaved woman living? She is living large. Fabulous women, powerful women, interesting women, Miss Behaved women, take up space. In this society, it is very Miss Behaved for a woman to take up more than the allotted four horizontal inches of area. That's why Miss Behaved women take up more, much more.

How can a woman make sure she is taking up enough space?

A quiz, requisite for all fine magazine articles.

Please answer Yes or No:

When you change into your carefully color-coordinated outfit for a torturous hour of aerobics at the Hard Metal Gym, do you try to use up no more than exactly one half of the bench placed in front of the lockers for your convenience, even though no one else is in the locker room?

When walking on the sidewalk, do you automatically step into the gutter to give the oncoming couple all the room so they can continue to walk shoulder to shoulder, hand to hand, hip to hip?

Do you hurry through checkout lines and bank lines because people are waiting behind you and they are in a hurry and their time must be more important than yours, so hurry up will you?

Answers:

If you answered yes to any one of these three questions, you are not taking up enough space.

There is a theory that the stronger and more independent women become, the less physical space it is fashionable for them to take up. Miss Behaved theorists believe that the creation of media-ready women, those skinny legged things on TV, is a direct and proportional response to the real-world power of women, as if women should compensate for their increase in power and knowledge by decreasing their physical shapes. The message is you cannot take up space and have power. Even though the former Prime Minister of England had the power, a bulimic princess got all the attention.

The Miss Behaved answer to that is—take both.

We encourage all women to not only take up space but, while they're at it, take over the boardroom. A Miss Behaved woman should strive to take up as many cubic feet in the room as possible, if not by virtue of size, then by virtue of a huge personality. Breathe deeply and use up all the oxygen. Learn to project your voice so that when you speak you suck up all the molecules in the thin air. Done well, a Miss Behaved woman will have so much command and presence that she will make those thin women look like, well, two-dimensional pictures.

Imagine this: a room filled with lovely young things, their dresses hanging from their bony shoulder blades so they look like nothing more than walking hangers. These women do not eat. They do not drink. They do not smile.

Enter, a fabulously Miss Behaved woman. She is dressed in a size 36 silver lame gown with a tiara on her bright red hair. She plows through those lovely young things, pushing them to the sides of the room like flotsam. She heads to the buffet table. She eats all the caviar. She smiles.

Big Miss Behaved women love fashion. They dress well, often in bright colors, eschewing black because how silly is it to think that black will make 230 pounds look thinner and why should anyone care?

And how is it that big Miss Behaved women have all this confidence? Shouldn't any woman who is not an immediate candidate for the cover of *Diets and Desserts Magazine* hide in shame until she purchases enough products to give her the appearance of being ready for her photo shoot?

Miss Behaved philosophy says no. Miss Behaved women have all this confidence, power, money, and authority because they do not waste their time trying to look like something they are not. They do not spend hours and hours each day working at being thin. They do not agonize over every bite of food before, during, and after every meal. They eat lunch; they get back to berating the board of directors.

Big Miss Behaved women will not be found hovering around the frozen food section in the grocery store wearing the same furtive expression found on men hovering anxiously around the entrance of a strip club. Miss Behaved women have needs, and those needs often involve pints of premium ice cream.

While the average skinny woman spends all her energy on the full-time activity of looking magazine-beautiful and television-thin, the Miss Behaved woman, clutching a bag of Circus Animal cookies, is taking over the world.

Don't be small. Be big.

The Fully Functional
Miss Behaved Home

The Miss Behaved Cook

◆

In a dramatic rescue sequence, best left to the imagination, I threw myself in front of my mother's left-over casserole and saved the family. It was difficult to choke down the last few bites of noodles and parsley, but I persevered and the family appreciated the conciliatory order of pad tai and curry.

The casserole in question was a left-over creation that my mother dropped off on her way to a cruise through the Panama Canal. My mother always cleans out her refrigerator prior to a lovely vacation that I can only experience through photos, and drops off any item from that refrigerator that is encased in Tupperware and still has some good left in it. Items often include two teaspoons of mustard/mayonnaise mix that can be used as a starter for salad dressing, three lettuce leaves, and a re-cycled plastic bag filled with dried parsley.

This casserole was 'really good chicken casserole' or, to be more true to my mother's shallowly planted culinary roots, 'a really good hot dish'. As the heiress to years of kitchen neglect I can now publicly acknowledge that there is a gap between my mother's enthusiasm in creating projects like the aforementioned 'really good chicken hot dish' and the bleak reality of the results.

In other words, my mother doesn't cook. Neither do I.

How did this happen? Shouldn't every woman cook? I asked this question and discovered, through shoddy research, that talent in cooking must originate from something or someone in order to manifest in the here and now.

My grandmother, the matriarch of this Miss Behaved family is a fine cook. No wait, she *had* a fine cook. She was excellent at engaging household help and truly brilliant at arranging dinner parties, but often she just called the Country Club and made reservations. Now 90 she keeps her dry cereal in the oven because there's so much room in there and it would otherwise be wasted space. She drives to the club should she need a roast beef dinner, steak, or a good highball.

Based on this evident inherited chain of incompetence, I developed the very Miss Behaved theory is that cooking is an inherited trait rather than strictly environmental.

I think that even if I was raised in one of those infamous families where young girls learn to hand roll ravioli in their grandmother's Tuscan kitchen, replete with Italian tiles and copper pots hanging from the ceiling, it still wouldn't take.

After sharing this theory with other like-minded Miss Behaved people, we have determined that I am right. It should also be noted that none of us find this in any way tragic.

Miss Behaved people are stalwart in their belief that cooking, the ability and the desire, is coded into a person's DNA. How else can we explain those people who wake up in the morning and their first thought is, "What are we fixing for dinner?" How else explain how and why some people get up at dawn, put on their bathrobe and slippers, trot out to the kitchen and load raw food into a crock pot, while the Miss Behaved person is only focused on finding the coffee because she can't remember, from morning to morning, where she put it? How else explain some people's uncanny ability to know which end of a green onion is eatable?

If scientists took a sampling of my own family's genetic material and stretched it out, they would discover that the codes normally dedicated to the impulse to read recipes for fun and to experiment with purple vegetables, have mutated to become the 1-800 number for Round Table Pizza. The large chicken garlic is our favorite.

But can't we poor starving Miss Behaved women overcome our own basic genetic make up and learn to apply heat to pots filled with liquid? Not when it's a very good excuse. Genetics is one of the best Miss Behaved excuses we've found for not doing something we already hate and are obviously not skilled in at all. Miss Behaved people who don't want to cook and don't have time to cook simply claim they cannot cook and have the carcasses of burned pans to prove it. If everyone could cook, take-out wouldn't have been invented.

And genetics is the only way to explain a recent Miss Behaved episode during which I tried to operate the oven in my brand new house all by myself. I could not figure out which button was the 'on' button (as if an oven is as easy to use as an iMac). I had no choice but to call my mother-in-law (who cooks) and ask how to program this thing. My mother-in-law, without ever seeing this oven, instructed me over the phone on not only how to turn it on, but also how to set the temperature and the timer.

That was the last time I tried to make a take-and-bake pizza.

Building the Miss Behaved Home

◆

The Miss Behaved theory of decorating is simple and straightforward. If the decorations in your house make you happy, that's good. If your décor makes your guests gasp in amazement, that's better. If your choice of furnishings and wallpaper keeps you up at night, you have achieved the ultimate Miss Behaved decorating goal.

The first step to achieving the perfect Miss Behaved home is to consider the basic architecture of your dream house. Most fine Miss Behaved architecture examples are not featured in handy design magazines, not even *Architectural Digest*. To get the right exposure, Miss Behaved dreamers must personally visit the more famous Miss Behaved homes and buildings.

There are two good examples of Miss Behaved architecture done in styles that just won't go away: The Winchester Mystery House and the Madonna Inn.

The Madonna Inn is a large, rambling tribute to one man's vision of the good life. The hotel is famous for its individually decorated theme rooms. One can stay in the Tack room, the Safari room, the Cave room, or if you wish to stay awake all night for whatever reason, the Canary room, painted a heart-stopping yellow. The architectural vision of this hotel is: if a cupola on top of a turret is good, then a cupola fitted in with green and red glass that glows like an indecisive stop light in the night is better. Most of the rooms are larger than many apartments.

As far as Miss Behaved analysts can determine, when something catches Mr. Madonna's eye, say a battery-operated plastic flower that changes colors continually in slow hypnotic movements, his immediate reaction is, "My that's pretty, order a hundred and entwine them through the gilded branches of the tree that spreads across the ceiling from the center of the steak house restaurant. The flowers will compliment the gold cupids hanging from the tree branches and the pink floral carpet that matches the pink tablecloths."

This is the correct Miss Behaved design attitude.

If you need an example of how to build many more additions and embellishments to your house than are strictly necessary, visit the Winchester Mystery House. Just the idea that a person can build and build and build without a single permit is thrilling to many Miss Behaved contractors and home owners. The concept of more is more and faster is faster is of course possible only if you are Sarah Winchester and are made of money and apparently little else. But we admire the way she built multitudes of rooms, wings and additions for reasons clear to only herself and her Ouija board.

Mrs. Winchester's home represents fine examples of conflicting architectural styles and demonstrates a wonderfully Miss Behaved way to spend money and enhance the ambiance of the neighborhood. You do not have to go as far as the Mystery House, but it is always possible to add a Queen Anne turret to the corner of a Craftsman style porch, then cap the whole affair with a red iron weathervane in the shape of a clipper ship.

Location, location, location. Just as the crest of the Industrial Age made it possible for robber barons to build larger than necessary homes, the crest of the new economy spawned the same Miss Behaved impulses. The charm of many of these grand Miss Behaved McMansions and gardens lies in the owners' complete disregard for place. This disregard accounts for large French villas in Cleveland and London Bridge in Arizona.

Instead of investing cash into a company that has no discernable product or service but does possess a colorful web site, a few forward thinking Miss Behaved capitalists sank that same amount of money into houses that will last for at least a generation and a half. And they are not sorry.

Before you build, remember that the whole point of a New Economy Dream House is to stand out. Like Miss Behaved visionaries before, create what you want and not only will praise and admiration come your way, but your neighbors will make special detours to see the house, if only to shock their out-of-town guests. Miss Behaved builders have many fine examples to choose from: a large Mediterranean villa complete with fountains and staggered terraces on the outskirts of a small ghost town in the Sierra foothills; a flat roofed Spanish style hacienda in the suburbs of Kansas City; or an awe-inspiring four-story brick townhouse in Los Angeles. One Miss Behaved individual insisted on recreating Waterfall House over a small summer stream in Wyoming. He rebuilds every spring after a torrent of melted snow carries last year's version down river.

The benefits of building in a Miss Behaved manner are not only that the house will be noticed, it will be more expensive. And, if you're very lucky, that brick house in LA will get you fifteen minutes of fame right after the next earthquake.

Which brings us to Miss Behaved space needs. If you are building a Miss Behaved house, make sure you don't create any building less than 10,000 square feet. A Miss Behaved rule of size is: if you don't need a schedule posted on the refrigerator (held there with those marvelous magnets that make noise, or play a little song) to visit each room in the house once a month, you haven't built a big enough house. Take a boat ride past Bill Gate's home for a New Economy example of excess.

Just as Mother Nature abhors a vacuum, the New Economy Miss Behaved home abhors sensible landscaping. Most McMansions are surrounded by environmentally inappropriate lawns but we do not recommend stopping there, although the ride-on mower is a tempting and necessary accompaniment to an acre of Kentucky blue grass. Set off your home, it's like creating the perfect filigree setting for a five-carat diamond. And it's not difficult. The simplest way to create a Miss Behaved environment is to completely disregard climate. Insist on nurturing tropical plants in the face of hostile weather, like a hibiscus bush in Connecticut, or cold weather flowers, like lilacs, in New Mexico.

If you can't nurture a garden that defies the laws of climate and local aesthetics, there is always gravel.

With a little ingenuity and a few carefully placed bribes to the planning department, you too can live in a completely Miss Behaved home. Consult your Ouija board for best location and style.

Dear Miss Behaved,
What should I wear to the wedding of my ex-boyfriend?
Signed,
Sigh of Relief

Dear Sigh,
If you are significantly thinner than the bride, wear a black sheath with no stockings and look fabulous. Try to talk with as many of the groom's friends as you can during the reception, so they can tell you what a big mistake he made by not marrying you.

Decorating

◆

There are many simple ways to get in touch with your Miss Behaved decorator.

We suggest starting small: install a faux waterfall that doubles as a urinal in the bathroom. Compliment this with a faux rock shower stall to give the impression that you are out in the wilds every time you shower. Or take inspiration from Graceland, a fine tribute to a man whose decorating taste was considered terribly Miss Behaved in his day and so had nothing to lose by doing exactly as he pleased. Compliment that rock lined-bath with a jungle-theme bedroom easily created by simply stapling faux leopard (do not kill your own leopards) fabric to the ceiling and tossing the remainder of the fabric onto the round queen-size bed. Add a couple of stuffed monkeys and you have a look.

For more sophisticated Miss Behaved decor, reference the honeymoon suites in the Poconos. The décor in these hotels is meant to evoke either love or fantasy, or the fantasy of love, but if you're that cynical, you're not honeymooning in the Poconos. To create the Miss Behaved memories of abandoned love and passion, we recommend installing large timber beams in the bedroom ceiling and red everywhere else. In the middle of the red-carpeted bedroom, place a large whirlpool champagne glass. It's bound to either bring back memories or create some new indelible ones.

Another quick and easy addition to the Miss Behaved home is a pool in the garage. You're not parking the car in there anyway; you may as well use it for something. For design inspiration, copy the indoor pool-room from Hearst Castle. Don't be too scrupulous in recreating every Julia Morgan detail; a half dozen plaster columns alternating between Corinthian and Doric should suffice to create the mood. Stencil a pattern on the bottom of the pool, add a Greek style border around the rim, and you have an instant classical touch that will compliment your Eichler home for years to come.

If you have a basement, install a pool table complete with regulation lighting. Include a bar with padded vinyl seats just like your favorite bar down the street, or even surreptitiously take those very stools, one at a time so no one notices. Hang your favorite art. You know the painting, dogs playing poker on velvet. Wallpaper should be flocked, carpets should be patterned because the remnant was on sale, and, voila, a Miss Behaved haven guaranteed to become the husband's exclusive sanctuary ever since his wife decorated the master bedroom with so much pink netting that if it were a room at the Madonna Inn, it would be called 'Princess Fantasy.' Every Miss Behaved couple should have their own rooms in the house anyway.

If you cannot afford to install a small personal pool in the center of the master bath, or if there's not enough room on your lot to upgrade your tract home into a Tudor mansion, do not despair. While Miss Behaved decorating is usually achieved by spending obscene amounts of money on questionable outcomes, one can decorate in a Miss Behaved way with items found around the house. Some are probably even wedding gifts.

Start small. A decorative wall plaque that sings when guests walk by is always a good Miss Behaved addition to any entryway. Fish, birds, and elephant heads singing clever songs like *Baby Elephant Walk* are all appropriate choices.

Pick a favorite decade and stick with it. If the seventies were good for you, keep the bean bag chairs, white shag carpeting, and series of neon-colored Grateful Dead posters positioned carefully under a black light. A few lava lamps scattered on low tables also provide a nice touch.

One Miss Behaved couple believes that it's only prudent to replace furniture when it wears out. Since the couple has always been very careful, the green high-low carpet, Danish modern furniture with avocado green vinyl upholstery and wrought-iron stair railings are still just like new. The plastic covers over the lamps was a good idea and the wife thanks her mother-in-law for that suggestion every Thanksgiving. There is no reason to replace perfectly good furniture. Besides, it's a well-known Miss Behaved fact that if you hold onto anything, it will either come back in style or you can get money for it on eBay.

A greatly admired Miss Behaved addition to the house, and one that is unassailable, is a large religious shrine dominated by a framed picture of the Virgin Mary dressed in blue with a large red heart beating at the center of her chest powered by faith and two 'D' batteries, set up in one corner of the formal living room.

Enhance the dining room table with a tall glass tower of shelves shaped like a pyramid that displays anything from Snow Baby figures to the complete collection of famous shoes carefully rendered in porcelain and hand numbered. To find enough small objects to fill large glass display cases, Hallmark stores are a treasure chest of Miss Behaved ideas. There is nothing more Miss Behaved than to devote an entire room to displaying useless but sentimental objects routinely purchased for this very purpose

A nice addition to the front hall is a large formal graduation photographs of the children that has been painted over so it looks like those classy portraits you admired on your last bus trip through Europe. At least one of the children should be riding a horse.

And of course, no Miss Behaved home should be without a few whimsical and brightly painted Disney dwarfs in the flowerbed. Plywood cutouts of people leaning over are also necessary installations in the Miss Behaved front and back yard. Do not use pink flamingos, because even though plastic flamingos are intrinsically Miss Behaved, too many cultured people have installed them as an ironic statement. Miss Behaved decorators are not trying to be ironic; Miss Behaved decorators are too busy setting up floodlights in the back yard (to highlight thirteen figures positioned to depict the final scene in *The Lion King*) to be ironic.

Inspired by extremely Miss Behaved motivations in an earlier life, one marvelously Miss Behaved couple displays the stuffed bodies and heads of now endangered species in the great room. A large African elephant head on the wall facing the front door greets guests and elephant tusks flank the fireplace. A stuffed snow leopard snarls over the big-screen TV. The second wife of this couple assures visitors that the husband is now very, very, sorry about his hunting years. But Miss Behaved guests are strangely drawn to the elephant tusks even as they feel repelled. Sure, we have seen hell for this man, and it looks like the African veldt, but we admire his chutzpa in not giving away the stuffed animals and keeping the bad karma all to himself.

He does not have any extra leopard skins for your bedroom, so forget it.

Miss Behaved Art
of Placemat, er, Placement

◆

Dear Miss Behaved,

I can't figure out where to put my Feng Shui books. Any Miss Behaved suggestions?

Signed,

Holding Heavy Books While Carefully Standing in the Driveway and Facing North West

Dear Standing,

Some people in our Miss Behaved household claim that Feng Shui is merely a horoscope for furniture. I disagree. I spent last Saturday, which my Psychic said was a good day for change, rearranging my house according to the principles listed in the three Feng Shui books in my possession. (I suggest just carrying them around from room to room for the time being).

Who hasn't been seduced by this current trend that promises instant wealth if one only places a plant with round leaves (round for coins) in the southeast corner of the main living space? Or a system that promises instant love is you set a candle, bell and a book (southwest, the kun sign) on the mantel? One book was little more than a compilation of success stories: people pulling themselves back from the brink of disaster by planting trees and building fountains. Outside. Unfortunately, everyone has their own Feng Shui disasters in their own way. And none of the house plans or problems resembled my own.

But I persevered because I was determined to capture or recirculate all the good Chi I could find. Not to confuse Chi with Chai which is tasty and worth circulating among friends.

The first book recommended fishing out the compass from my youngest child's Junior Explorer Save the Wild Life Fund Kit and marking the compass points inside the house that correspond to the Bagua Map on page 38. So I walked around my house with a compass and the map deflecting comments from my spouse about being lost in the dining room. I dutifully identified the southwest and east corners and walls of my house by marking the walls northwest or southwest because every time I set down the compass it moved a little to the left.

I stood outside and squinted at the sun, guessing, after much twisting and turning, that the house was a west house. A west house is good for me, according to calculations listed on page seven of book two that required too much math, because I am a west person. But a west house is bad for my spouse because, after further inaccurate math, I discover that he is an east person. All this time I thought he was from Marin.

According to book three, one's house should have high dragon hills to the left, with low tiger hills (that should not at any cost be disturbed), to the west. Roads past the ferocious sleeping tiger should be avoided. There should be black turtle hills right behind the house and a crimson phoenix right in front. I live in a $350,000 tract home, nestled up against three other tract homes none of which resemble a tiger. The most auspicious feature of my home is that it's only 10 minutes away from Macy's. Depressed, I gesture to the Chi to at least come inside and enjoy the three red wind chimes I just purchased from the Feng Shui store located just over the mountains that don't resemble much of anything.

Once inside I look up the meanings of each area of the house. The front hall and door are east and are responsible for family and health. The dog run is north, in the career prospects. In the second book, the Pa Kua circle is skewed so the front door of any building or room is at the northern point. According to this book then, the front door is in the career prospects area and the dog run in the luck part of the house. Either way the dog is pissing on something important.

The third book strongly cautioned against keeping a toilet in the wealth (sign of the Sun, number six, facing the dragon mountains across the tiger hills) corner of the house. This could be a problem as moving around a toilet to the best part of the house according to conflicting maps is not, for the most part, feasible. Even if one's husband is a plumber.

In fact, according to all three books, toilets are bad for the flow of Chi no matter where they are placed. The toilet cannot be placed anywhere within an important or auspicious area of the house, and most areas in the house are important and/or auspicious, so terrible choices have to be made. Do you flush down the Chi of marital happiness, or do you flush down the Chi of prosperity, or do you flush away the children? And really, most of us consider inside toilets to be good, and that they consistently flush to be even better.

The argument (according to the books) is that when all this was figured out, the ancient kings did not have toilets in the house. This might have been good Feng Shui then, but nowadays keeping the toilet out side means the family has fallen on pretty hard times. We could even go so far as to predict that a toilet outside is very bad Chi. Look what happened to the lawyer in *Jurassic Park*.

My toilet is inside sort of to the left in the lower southwest corner of the center of the house which is the family and children part, which makes sense because even when I'm in the bathroom, the children still don't leave me alone.

Exhausted from carrying these books from room to room, book three is in hardcover, I decided that the best thing is not to worry about the family, but find the most auspicious place in the house for me to sit. I am the Mother, western, number two, element: anxiety.

According to the Lo Shu grid in book one, the most auspicious place for me in the house is the southern corner but before I sit down, I read further to discover that the corner also represents children, as in more. Oh sure, if you work a farm on a daily basis and don't mind about the bad chi in the outhouse.

I eyed the auspicious corner for another second or two, and decided to ignore it since we can't afford any more children let alone more Game Boys. I place the books in the pile of manuals and guide books to Diablo II and Dungeons and Dragons (not the auspicious kind) in the soft glow of the downstairs computer because computers are not mentioned in any of the three books so I've decided they qualify as neutralizing elements. I use the bathroom with no dire consequences that I can see, hang the wind chimes in the garage, and lie down in the middle of the house, where the dog steps on my face.

The right answer must be blowing in the Chi.

Behind the Scene
at Lofty Home Magazine

◆

A transcript of a Miss Behaved conversation during a photo shoot for *Lofty Home Magazine* slipped through the rank and file and landed on the Internet. Three Miss Behaved readers downloaded it and passed it along, not because they are mean spirited, but because they always suspected there was more to that fine shelter magazine copy than was allowed to pass through the editorial department and on to the gullible readership.

Miss Behaved readers are familiar with these beautiful and evocative magazines. We love to read magazines like *Lofty Home Magazine, Architecture Everywhere* and *House, Home and Driveway* because in our Miss Behaved hearts we know that the homes and advice featured in these elaborate shelter magazines are about as realistic as the profile of last month's Playmate of the Year (biggest turn on, walks on the beach with her special guy). What PhotoShop work is to *Playboy*, camera angles, styling and astute editorial copy are to shelter magazines. Today we offer Miss Behaved proof.

Our Miss Behaved conversation took place during the photo shoot of a 'typical American home'. It was reported that this conversation began immediately after three photo stylists finished rescuing strange and unusual items from all over the house to put in the kitchen. They added a few plastic vegetables from the well stocked *Lofty Home Magazine* van parked out front, and piled the entire collection of disparate things onto the kitchen counters.

"Kitchen counters look like airport runways in photographs." the stylist explained to the understandably curious homeowners, Frank and Mike. She ruched a linen towel on the left side of the counter, plopped a vase of tulips in the sink, and mounded a clutch of photogenic leeks onto the middle of the breakfast bar.

It was only after they recovered from the initial shock of seeing tulips in the sink that the couple, who conceptualized and financed the innovative poured cement counters and Italian tiled floor with radiant heating for those 'chilly mornings', discussed how they would be portrayed in the article.

"Listen," said Mike, "my mother reads this magazine; her whole damn bridge club reads this magazine. So, since I am the creative member of this couple, I get to be the cook."

"Mike is the gourmet cook in the house." he dictated to the copywriter who was too busy fingering the leeks and making suggestive remarks to one of the stylists to write it down.

"But you're not a gourmet cook," Frank protested. "I'm the gourmet cook. I took the classes at the Culinary Institute. You were too busy with your career. In fact, if I recall correctly, the last time we entertained your parents, you spooned Chinese onto the good china and pretended it was a recipe you picked up during your last trip to Hong Kong. And you've never been to Hong Kong."

"Yes, but periodicals are forever," intoned Mike, "therefore, I get to be the gourmet cook."

"Okay, big guy," Frank challenged, "then where is the colander?"

What followed was pregnant silence. The copywriter had abandoned the leeks and all hope of impressing the stylist. She was squinting at the Polaroids and complimenting the photographer. The third stylist looked expectantly at the pretender to the Betty Crocker crown. The crown prince puzzled about it for a minute or two, then his face cleared.

"Isn't it that helmet thing that guy wore when he contacted Mulder during the third season of *X-Files* and told him that the Aliens were trying to send radio signals directly into his brain?"

"Close, we'll say we are both gourmet cooks."

"Busy," the copywriter then piped up. "You are both busy with your demanding careers but the spacious kitchen is perfect for this couple who enjoys cooking gourmet meals together on the weekend."

"Why busy?" asked the Frank, suspiciously eyeing his lounging partner.

"Well," returned the copywriter diplomatically, "you were busy figuring out where the colander was."

The published article was a smashing success, and no one in Mike's mother's bridge club asked the relevant question; why are all remodeled Connecticut farmhouses owned by couples with names like Frank and Mike? But two members of the bridge club did inquire about the leeks scattered on the breakfast bar, as Frank is allergic.

Another wonderfully Miss Behaved feature in the annals of stylish periodicals is the designer house that purportedly houses children. Miss Behaved readers figure that these children are either fictitious, created to cover up something terribly amiss in the partnership of the home-owners, or they are away at boarding school.

Take the profile of a couple featured in *Home, Field and Stream* who just re-decorated their cozy 4,500 square foot house with space-saving appliances and an open floor plan to give the house a more expansive feeling. The copy on page 119 explained that "Since they now have a toddler, Phyllis and George have slip covered the couch in a rough-and-tumble light beige silk. Their collection of priceless ceramic objects with sharp edges has been edited down to the bare minimum of 37 and is now kept on low three-legged tables imported from Thailand."

"The white wool carpets are so easy to keep clean," explained Phyllis. "We think it lightens the room to have all white with only a dash of color from our irreplaceable Venetian glass collection we house in this glass shelving unit that stands about five inches away from the wall and will tip in even the slightest breeze."

When the stylist asked where the toddler was kept since a small child was the perfect size to "balance the couch, otherwise they look like long runways", the couple looked around for a bit, but then had to admit they seemed to have misplaced the child and could a suitable child photo be inserted during post production? "That way there will be more control over the look," George explained.

Another Miss Behaved couple featured in *Lofty Home Magazine* was justifiably proud of their new space. The family room was really a large loft space complete with refinished, then stressed, wood floors and little else. The stylist placed a hand-carved Swedish table and chair painted in bright primary colors in the center of the room "to warm it up".

The couple was quoted as saying that their lovely little five-year-old Zoë "just loves to put all her toys away in these color coded bins from Scandinavia. Why, she's as neat and tidy as we are!"

It is the Miss Behaved opinion that Zoë will eventually rebel and move into a re-furbished lighthouse with a couple named Stan and Rich.

Dear Miss Behaved,
What does the definitive Miss behaved kitchen look like?
Signed,
Subscriber to *House and Garden*

Dear Garden,
A feature on the Miss Behaved kitchen is scheduled to appear in the November issue of the popular Miss Behaved periodical *Diets and Desserts*.

The copy reads, "This busy Miss Behaved mother depends on the highest of high tech equipment to feed her voracious children who have often been mistaken for gorillas during a feeding frenzy. While making the best of the embedded traditional fixtures that apparently come with every home, she is more than just quick and efficient, she makes use of the updated state-of-the—art equipment newly installed in the kitchen and does so to great effect."

The photo pictures a close up of the cell phone with maybe a basket of take-out menus and fast food coupons on the side, so the counter won't look like a runway.

A Miss Behaved Holiday

◆

During the holidays, it is fashionable to denigrate poor Martha worth-a-billion-dollars Stewart. One Miss Behaved woman remembers accidentally watching an early Martha Stewart program in the mid-eighties. For Thanksgiving dinner, Martha hollowed out a pumpkin, gilded it, and used it as a centerpiece filled with savory homemade pumpkin soup. The early Miss Behaved reaction was "What the hell is she doing?"

The answer is building an empire. However, it is quite possible to admire the net worth of the messenger while still ignoring the message.

That established, how does the Miss Behaved women go about creating a festive party atmosphere for her family, set a holiday table that could be photographed for the cover of *Victoria* magazine, complete complicated end-of-the-year tasks at work, shuffle the children to extra rehearsals, attend lengthy sports awards ceremonies in which her child will be called on last, and winterize the dog, all in a month's time?

She doesn't.

Since the pages of a Miss Behaved missive are the only place you will find this kind of advice; we'll put it right here. She doesn't; they don't; we don't.

True Miss Behaved holiday entertaining does not include gilt pumpkins or charming mismatched china place settings. In fact, that special holiday glow we see on the faces of magazine-mothers may not, after all, be the indirect light achieved by placing beeswax candles on every available surface. It may just be the flush of exertion.

What, then, does a Miss Behaved holiday house look like? How can you tell if you're headed down that Miss Behaved path of incompetent (but relaxed) holiday entertaining? If your reaction to the suggestion that candles add a touch of excitement and novelty to the house for the holidays is, they certainly do. Candles beckon my three boys to plunge their chubby fingers directly into the hot wax and create those novel wax covered fingers, perfect for startling Grandma. And most of us admit that when the holly centerpiece caught fire, it was very exciting. Then you've already embraced salient Miss Behaved holiday concepts.

The first thing Miss Behaved entertaining guides suggest is to ditch the beeswax candles. Real candles are easily replaced with plastic candles complete with tiny electric light bulbs in the shape of flames. Without the candles, decorating becomes easier and less prone to flare-ups.

Some Miss Behaved people even go as far as treating Christmas as the birthday celebration that it is. They decorate with leftover birthday streamers and lights in the shape of little pieces of cake, both of which are appropriate, and if positioned right, artistic. The plastic cake lights can be strung in between the plastic evergreen garlands on the stairs. Paint the extension cord green and drape it elegantly along the remainder of the wall. No one will notice.

Another Miss Behaved suggestion for holiday entertaining is to only entertain people you really, really, love, since that way you won't have to decorate much at all. Every Miss Behaved women knows that we only decorate to impress strangers. True friends don't care. Ask guests to bring extension cords and more lights.

Serve take-out food. This is so obvious we won't even elaborate except to say that if you spent $250 at Safeway this month and have a club card and win a turkey just in time for the holidays, then for heaven's sake make sure the bird is cooked, stuffed, and comes with all the 'fixins'. This strategy ensures that there will be plenty of room left in the kitchen to pour and mix drinks. A heavily spiked eggnog is key to a festive holiday evening. Guests will either become extremely happy and forgetful, or pass out—both good Miss Behaved options.

Begin the evening with the one bottle of good wine left in the cellar and switch to the cheap wine during dinner. If you are feeling even a little like Martha Stewart, you can spend your weekend steaming off the wine labels from the good wine and sticking them onto the cheap wine. Not as easy as it looks, is it? If you were more gifted, it would be an easy project taking up no more than five hours of your time. But then again, if you were gifted, you'd be worth more and wouldn't have to do this at all.

Paper goods are an important component to Miss Behaved entertaining. Oh sure, many Miss Behaved women picked up some expensive china during an elaborate wedding or two, and we suggest displaying that place setting on the mantle for the new in-laws to admire. But for any event that involves cleaning up afterwards, buy festive paper products. For Christmas, pull out the plates and cups printed with pumpkins, witches or birthday clowns. It demonstrates that they are recycled and/or bought on sale and you are a thrifty sort of person.

Another excellent Miss Behaved survival tactic for the holidays is to exchange competencies. It's not hard for a Miss Behaved woman to figure out her talents; they are few and easy to count off on one hand. Trade what you know about reaching the last mile in telecommunications with a friend who has three good cookie recipes and is willing to whip up a batch of each for you. One Miss Behaved woman bid on homemade cookies at an auction and supplied her family nicely all through the holidays. Another Miss Behaved woman decided that the bakery next to her house was close enough to claim they were nearly homemade and picked up a couple of dozen every week in December.

Some Miss Behaved people have observed that every year the neighbors are compelled to spend a great deal of money for the privilege of dragging an ant infested tree from the wilds of the tree farm into their nice clean house. They then spend hours carefully decorating it with elaborate hand-blown glass ornaments, knowing that the look in the dog's eye does not bode well for the health of the project. But they insist, year after year. Since Miss Behaved people sometimes lose all sense of purpose during the holidays, they too drag in a tree and dutifully decorate it.

But Miss Behaved tree decorators eschew the fancy glass ornaments in favor of completely covering the tree with fake snow from a can. Some Miss Behaved children try to bring in the snow from outside, but it often doesn't look as nice since they found the snow under the car and it's a bit dirty (the snow as well as the car). Ornaments depicting the children's favorite cartoons, thirteen pounds of silver tinsel, and a few green plastic balls complete the Miss Behaved look. A few very Miss Behaved families decorate a fake tree with happy birthday banners and chili pepper lights.

While in the throes of shopping, decorating, scooping out pumpkins and buying cans of pumpkin soup, some Miss Behaved people must listen to other very sincere people attempt to point out that the real meaning of Christmas is the birth of our savior. The secondary meaning of Christmas is family, which often involves spending an entire weekend with estranged members of your spouse's side who you wouldn't ordinarily hail on the street (the family members, not your spouse).

Miss Behaved people acknowledge the big-picture sentiment and choose instead to celebrate the holidays by missing Mass, forgetting to send cards to relatives they don't like, giving the last of the purchased gingerbread house to the dog, throwing handfuls of fake snow at one another during the big holiday meal and accidentally igniting a sibling's tennis shoe in the rush to be first to gather all the wrapping paper in order to create a bigger bonfire in the fireplace than we had last year.

These same sincere people attempt to counter this disastrous Miss Behaved attitude by praying vigorously for the Miss Behaved family during this holiday season. Miss Behaved people are grateful for this effort. On the other hand, they know that their contribution to the holidays is to give well-behaved people something neutral to discuss during their own tense relative-laden holiday meal. Miss Behaved families; their indoor snow, the birthday banners, the story of the burning tennis shoe, are far more interesting than explaining how to get the soup to stay in the pumpkin.

Vacuuming Woman
—a Performance Piece

◆

Everything can be turned into art. Tragic childhoods become novels. Crime is turned into television specials. What were once considered acts of vengeance and gross negligence are now considered talk-show fodder.

In this cold exploitative atmosphere, what is a Miss Behaved artist to do? How does one push the boundaries when there is no line left to cross?

Miss Behaved experts and art historians recommend that Miss Behaved artists jump off the cutting edge, which is not only narrow and sharp but difficult to balance on for very long, and look instead inward.

Vacuuming Woman is the new, new thing. This piece is inherently inclusive. Many artists won't even have to leave their quiet homes to appreciate and enjoy the breadth of this work. This work is so Off-Off-Broadway it's in the living room.

The piece opens with a spotlight trained on a single woman. She wears her most comfortable leggings, the ones with the twice mended crotch. She knows she should throw them out, but Target isn't selling this brand anymore and they don't cling to her burgeoning thighs the way other brands do. She wears a tee-shirt from a volunteer project she participated in three years ago. Some of the corporate sponsors displayed on the back of the shirt have since gone out of business.

The woman is barefoot, the better to feel the mess beneath her feet.

She enters the living room, the heart of the house, the place where the family should be nurtured and loved and play games together every

Thursday night, 'Family Game Night', but instead consistently suc-
cumbs to watching reruns of *Who's Line is it Anyway?*.

The archetypal woman sighs as she surveys her crumb-strewn abode.
She grimaces with anguish. She furrows her brow with despair. She
wonders who authorized the eating of popcorn, the making of toast, the
brushing of dog.

The atmosphere is brown and dusty, the curtains are closed because
the Vacuuming Woman hasn't yet transformed into the Window
Washing Woman, and isn't likely to anytime soon.

Suddenly a new spotlight illuminates The Vacuum.

This, she thinks with naïve enthusiasm, will solve the crumb and dust
problem. This promises to completely eliminate the black dog hair from
the mint green couch. This, she thinks, her frown smoothing, will solve
all my distress and anguish and then I can rest.

With care, she bends, feeling the stitches in the crotch of her leggings
give just a little more than they should, and plugs the machine into the
wall plug. The goal, the art, is to vacuum as far into the house as she can
from that single plug because, once the vacuuming rhythm is established, it's too much trouble to stop, pull the plug, and reinsert into a
new location. Last week she had to do that and chipped a nail on the
baby-safe outlet cover.

With a satisfying roar the vacuum starts to life. It's only after the vacuum starts up that she remembers she has no more bags and this one is
full. Her choices at this critical juncture are: throw out and replace the
bag, necessitating a trip out to the garbage (see *Garbage Walk Number 6*
in the program), or empty the bag and reuse it, thus saving a few pen-
nies, or assume that like any other resource, more room will be made in
the bag's interior if she just persists. She persists.

The roar engulfs her and only a little bit of dust blows out from the
back of the machine. Machine and woman become one in the pursuit of
popcorn kernels, dust, and that purple thread that will not be swept up
by the vacuum brushes. She pauses next to a trash can, leans over, feels

more give in her leggings, and manually feeds the thread to the Vacuum's maw. Together they sweep over dingy carpet, leaving a clean swath of back-brushed pile in their wake.

The black vacuum cord whips around each corner of every room, leaving a dark mark that will never come out until the women repaints the whole house in anticipation of selling. Any corner that is not reached by the vacuum tethered to that carefully chosen single outlet is ignored. All messes are made in the middle of the floor anyway. The dog only throws up in the center of the carpet, not on the edges where at least the stains can be hidden in creative and decorative ways (see *Woman and her Spot Remover* in the program).

The woman pushes the roaring vacuum; the vacuum responds to her commands. The noise of the vacuum blocks out all outer disturbances. While the Vacuuming Woman works, she can tune out all external distractions—the phone with solicitation calls, the door bell with solicitation demonstrations, the children soliciting for another juice box even though there's a perfectly good pitcher of drinks in the refrigerator. The Vacuuming Woman hears nothing.

She cleans, therefore she is. The Vacuuming Woman creates a safe cocoon of purpose, focus, and noise. She works carefully on the carpet in methodical back and forth movements. She switches to attachments and works over the couch, the chairs, a few swipes at the blinds. But even as she reaches the end of the power cord, even as she makes the supreme effort to move at least two chairs and actually vacuum entirely under them, we sense, as she works, that this is not permanent. Even the artist knows this, her innate knowledge of the futility of cleaning a carpet that is regularly abused is reflected in her avoidance of the stair treads. There is not enough dirt to justify lifting the vacuum from tread to tread. She makes difficult choices.

As she pulls the plug and rolls the vacuum with the overflowing bag to the closet, she only allows a few minutes of self-congratulation. The artist knows that this work, this piece, is a tribute to the continuing effort displayed by vacuuming women everywhere and it will not last.

We too sense, as we watch, that there is no end, there is just always the vacuum.

Applause comes only from the artist herself.

Husbands and Lovers

The Stunt Husband

---◆---

Dear Miss Behaved,

I don't understand it. My husband won't go with me to the concert, won't go with me to the new German play and has never, ever volunteered to come with me to a poetry reading at our local bookstore. I didn't know he would be so difficult when I married him, what should I do?
Signed,
Missing Art (not my husband's name)

Dear Missing,

Every Miss Behaved wife has a Star husband, the main man, the person who puts the 'community' into property. However, like most artists, this Star husband can be quirky, moody and very often will do anything to avoid doing dangerous scenes that are part of life. Begging him to do so because the close-up will look more realistic is pointless. The tabloids are rife with stories of Star husbands who refused to show up for museum openings, the formal wedding of a second cousin, and that class in Hindu tapestry weaving.

The Miss Behaved wife, however, will not accept the lame excuse "I'll be in my trailer" or "I have to practice for a big scene at the office tomorrow." She wants company, she wants it now, and she wants someone else to pay for drinks.

But it is never wise to make a valuable Star perform beyond his range. We recommend you get a stunt.

For instance, you probably contracted with the Star husband long before you realized he couldn't dance. After carefully editing the wedding video so it looks as if you, the bride, was happily dancing with the Star (when actually it was your cousin Bert wearing the groom's tuxedo jacket), you may have realized, like many Miss Behaved wives, that you better find a good substitute. Because there are many scenes in a Miss Behaved life that require a male dancing partner.

Miss Behaved wives who like to dance do not wait around for the Star to figure out that dancing is romantic, take private lessons, and surprise her one evening at the local beer hall with his new moves. He would never think to do that because he refuses to watch the dozen or so films like *Dirty Dancing* or *Strictly Ballroom* that would show him how to move, if not like a pro, then at least well enough to not be a danger to others. So you need a Stunt husband to do the dancing.

The Wedding Stunt husband is the easiest to find. A Miss Behaved woman can either take a friend to the wedding or borrow a brother-in-law who is already at the wedding, is bored and who loves to dance. In either case, the Stunt should have the stamina to do dancing scenes with both his own wife and the Miss Behaved woman. Most Star husbands will not be jealous. In fact they look upon this missed opportunity to do the Chicken Dance with great serenity. Saved from certain tragedy on the dance floor, the Star sits on the sidelines, smiles for the photographer and drinks another screwdriver while the Stunt husband steps in and steps out and flaps his arms. Payment for this work usually comes in six packs.

Our favorite movies aside, even Miss Behaved women know it's not all about dancing. For instance, one Miss Behaved wife took her brand new Star husband to the Modern Art Museum. He patiently trailed behind her while she exclaimed and admired many paintings that he secretly thought were silly but, since the honeymoon wasn't quite over, he held his tongue. It wasn't until they happened across a magnificent hanging Calder mobile that he balked, then had a flash of inspiration. He claimed that, in San Francisco, standing under something like a mobile was dangerous. The slightest tremor would cause the artwork to crash down and crush him. It was too great a risk.

"No," he said, "I can't put you through that kind of anguish." Thus, he concluded, no more Modern Art Museums visits for the Star.

It was brilliant and purely Miss Behaved logic. Feeling he was in the zone and now would be a good time to continue contract negotiations, he also commented on the season tickets she held for the ballet. He was very concerned with the relative height of the balcony seats in the War Memorial Opera house.

"Those seats are pretty high up", he said, "A Star could lose his footing and tumble to his death, you know."

"Yes," she mused, "a Star could tumble to his death. But it would be quick."

Plus he had just written all the insurance polices in her favor, but that is another Miss Behaved solution. For today, we are concentrating on keeping the Star husband around.

So what did this Miss Behaved wife do? Did she insist her husband shape up and love all that she loved? Did she drag the Star to every program during the season just so he could crinkle his program and complain loudly during intermission that he just didn't get it?

Taking Miss Behaved advice, she found a Stunt husband. In this case, her Stunt husband had the added advantage of holding a lifetime contract with her as official best friend. And he can dance.

This friend, in fact, embodies all the important features and job competencies for the perfect Stunt husband. He will never marry and become the Star husband himself. His serious relationships accommodate a long-time female friend who needs (and wants) escort to art events, window shopping at Restoration Hardware and lengthy conversations about esoteric ideas and concepts that always sounded a bit pretentious to the Star.

He has the same taste in men. He looked great in their high school twentieth reunion photograph. He will always be single.

Long term Stunt husbands need to be single.

The Star husband, in turn, is delighted with the new arrangement. Because a Stunt has taken over, the Star can stay at home doing Star activities: helping with the kid's homework, cleaning the kitchen after making dinner, picking up the house, watching *Comedy Central*, all in the comfort of his Star-quality environment.

Meanwhile the Stunt husband braves the Grand Tier and buys his loaner wife expensive truffles during intermission.

As she matures, a Miss Behaved woman acquires a number of professional helpers in her life—hairdressers, manicurists, massage therapists, psychotherapists, color consultants, lawyers, doctors, grips, best boys. Why not a Stunt husband as well?

The Stunt saves wear and tear on the Star by doing dangerous deeds, like risking a chance encounter with a tipsy Benjamin Moore sculpture and sitting through the world premiere of *Schaubühne am Lehniner Platz*. In its entirety. The Stunt can execute a scene in which the couple attempts to parallel park in Berkeley without damaging the relationship or the car. The Stunt won't discuss the specifics of the oldest child's last report card or why the youngest child can't manage to land the dishes in the dish washer. He doesn't care, and in fact must be reminded of the children's ages. The Stunt doesn't even need the wardrobe mistress; he dresses for the part all by himself.

A good Stunt husband ensures that the Star relationship will always remain stable and satisfactory. For instance, when one Miss Behaved wife came home from a particularly fine ballet performance, thrilled with the exactitude of movement, thrilled with discussing the performance using really big words, the Star husband raised his head and sleepily asked, "Who won?"

Keep the Star around because he matches the children and that makes for a nicer looking family Christmas photo. But for serious work in the arts, get a Stunt.

The Second Wife Be One Now!

◆

It all started at book club. The club members had read this rather benign book about an elderly man who, as soon as his first wife died, shocked his family and the town citizens by marrying a much younger woman.

In the book, the first wife raised the children, did without, supported her husband through the lean times by doing without, looked dour and ugly because she spent all her energy sacrificing and doing without. Then she died and received a small funeral, still doing without to the end.

The second wife was young and good-looking, owned nice clothes, purchased more nice clothes, wore hats, remodeled the house, got a car, received gifts, acquired electricity.…You get the picture.

A truly Miss Behaved moment emerged from this seemingly benign book. One of the book club members slammed the book closed and declared, "That's it! I'm going to be the second wife!"

That night she explained to her husband (a patient man), "Peter (his real name) pretend I died." She let that sink in for about a second. "Now," she continued, "pretend I'm your new, young, second wife. Now, here's what I want."

To date, she has purchased a larger house, engaged a housekeeper, upgraded her job, and returned to school to get her Ph.D. She looks younger. She is happier. She recommends becoming the second wife to any woman she cares deeply about.

The first wife puts off her career to raise the kids, cleans the house herself, rearranges old furniture to give the house a 'new' look, and works endless hours to launch whatever venture the couple decides upon. The first wife supports, does without, and trains the husband to cook, clean, and be sensitive to women's issues.

Now, the book club members aren't saying this isn't the right thing to do. In fact, it's the natural course of events. The first wife thoughtfully writes the first chapter of the couple's life, she labors under the smaller income of a young family; she works hard. The rub is this: the second wife often appears on the scene at a more prosperous time (usually after the kids are out of college with more household income and fewer children at home) just when those little gifts of diamonds are affordable. What the book club members agreed on is that they all wanted to be part of that second, prosperous chapter in a couple's life.

Before all you second wives howl to Dear Abby, or at the moon, and claim that you have it just as bad as the first wife, or actually worse since you must tolerate the first wife's children (who weren't raised correctly at all), please understand that this concept has nothing to do with you. This is not about new husbands, blended families, or falling in love again. This is about the same relationship moving into the next Miss Behaved phase.

The members of this Miss Behaved book club do not want new husbands. On the contrary, they love the husbands they have. Besides, they're trained. What this group of Miss Behaved women wants is the glorious second half of the marriage. They want the second-wind relationship. They want to be the 'new wife', there when the hard-working, bread-winning, successful husband comes up for air (sometime in his forties) and says, "Hey, I need to get a life." And the new, 'second wife' will reply, "You're right, and I've already booked the flight to Tahiti."

Second wives book flights to Tahiti. Original wives, because of years of training, fret about wasting the money when they could be purchasing cars for the children.

"Enough," say the newly second wives, "it's time for us, and it's time for some fun."

So much of the first part of marriage is built on making due. The first marriage is built from countless moments of eating 99 cent specials in the Burger King parking lot a foot from the bumper of the van filled with sleeping children who, if they stay asleep, won't ask for all the French fries.

As the couple maintains their original marriage they forget that, if they aren't careful or if the Miss Behaved wife is not diligent, the second half of the marriage will look, feel, and taste exactly like the first. Miss Behaved women realize that they do not have to stay in this first self-sacrificing gear forever. They can shift to second gear, pull out of the parking lot, and do it in a new sports car.

One book club member decided to take the second-wife theory even further. She plans to become a trophy wife.

First, her husband has to be able to afford her, so she meets regularly with her stockbroker, tax accountant, and lawyer to plan for effective retirement and estate management. Second, she is training the first husband in appropriate trophy wife appreciation. She tapes DeBeers ads and plays them during breaks in whatever game he's watching on TV. She takes him on field trips to Gumps and Tiffany.

Her next step is to have most of her parts enhanced, including a new hydraulic system installed into her chest. She dyed her hair blond and got herself a career. Since trophy wives not only belong, but have time to attend a gym, she signed up and made the time. She learned about out-of-the-way vacations that do not include free mouse ears, and brushed up on restaurants, wine, and gourmet take-out services.

Since part of the trophy wife's job is to belong to the right clubs and work on the correct fundraising projects, this Miss Behaved first wife signed up early. Now instead of supporting her husband by doing without, turning down the heat, and making birthday party favors out of coffee filters and food coloring, this trophy wife risks her hard-won figure by attending endless charity luncheons.

Mindful that trophy wives are often willing to take up activities that the original wife rejected as silly and a waste of time, this newly minted trophy wife took up golf. She compensated for the ridiculousness of the game by purchasing darling little outfits and flirting with the golf pro.

This former first wife reports that the only catch in remaking herself into the trophy wife is that trophy wives indulge the 'new' husband in all things. This is sometimes problematic, as indulging often requires staying awake past ten o'clock and a willingness to participate in strenuous activities in the late evening hours.

It was this part of the trophy wife program that finally captured the first husband's imagination. He stopped complaining about the DeBeers cartel and the new graphite-handled golf clubs and embraced his new trophy wife with vigor not seen since they first dated.

The book club members never said this would be easy.

Dear Miss Behaved,

I am a healthy 160-pound woman, but the number 160 is not acceptable in our society. Is there a Miss Behaved solution to my problem?

Signed,

Not Giving up the Pizza

Dear Perfect Size 12,

Certainly, tell people you used to weigh 240 pounds and have dieted rigorously to achieve your current weight. Nothing is more impressive than strict self-denial—it's very Puritan and very American. And of course working from false assumptions is far easier and more Miss Behaved than actually doing something about the reality of your situation. So walk along the beach in the smallest swimsuit you can struggle into and if anyone remarks on your size or, worse, gives you one of those 'looks' cheerfully exclaim, "Can you believe it! Just last year I was wearing a pup tent!"

It's so much better to create the illusion of sacrifice than to actually do the work.

Miss Behaved
at a High School Reunion

───────────── ◆ ─────────────

Dear Miss Behaved,

For twenty years I've wondered. Does winning Homecoming Queen in your Senior year of high school guarantee eternal happiness?

Signed,

Second Runner Up

Dear Runner,

No. I'll tell you why.

At my husband's high school reunion, I sat at the Homecoming Court table. In high school I couldn't even get my sorry dateless body to any homecoming game, let alone the dance, let alone be considered a candidate for the Homecoming Court, yet here we all were. The real guests had no idea I didn't belong at their table. Ironically, many people who meet me for the first time erroneously suspect that I was indeed a cheerleader, but I believe it's because 'pep', so valuable in high school, is a trait often attributed to adults who are simply loud.

I was fascinated with these women. Twenty years ago, not a single one of them would have even bothered to greet me in the Girls Room, not even if I was sitting in the stall with the last of the toilet paper. Twenty years later, I not only looked just like them, I was offered, unbeknownst to them, the opportunity to answer the Miss Behaved question: is being a member of the homecoming court as fabulous as girls claimed? Did these chosen girls, the most popular in the school and favored by the football team (who voted on who would be a princess and ultimately queen of homecoming) grow up to have different lives than the normal people? Were they truly, as I believed 20 years ago, better than the rest of us?

I introduced myself as the wife of the guy to my left, the editor of the school paper and the student body vice president (the president was sitting at table six), but not a member of the football team (which meant he still had use of his original knees). Three of the women nodded in his direction. One (we'll call her Christine because that's close to her real name) wasn't paying attention to any guests except for Julie Robinski, sitting directly across from her.

Christine was still working on some homecoming issues. The biggest issue was that she, Christine, was not crowned queen and Julie Robinski was.

To my left, Lisa, who sympathized with Christine's pain, wasn't mad at Julie Robinski for winning the coveted crown, but vividly remembered what it felt like to lose.

"There you are," she explained to me in hushed tones, "standing in the middle of a football field, surrounded by hundreds of people. You have to wave to them all and smile, all the while thinking 'Hi, thank you. Yes, I'm the loser, member of the court, not the queen, loser, just a princess, no pictures please'. And," she continued, "we all had to ride around the football field in these cars donated by Hansen Ford Trucks and the guys driving the cars were the student body officers. We were all in this line and had to climb into the cars as soon as the ceremony was over. I think I ended up with the historian. And I still had to wave." She shuddered at the memory, either of having to wave or of having to sit so close to the historian who, by nature of that elected post, is usually a total geek and possibly a member of the school band.

And the queen? Did winning that coveted tiara (that was becoming more jewel-encrusted with every passing minute according to Christine) change Julie's life? Julie Robinski did not say.

Christine, however, did say. As she gulped her third glass of passable Merlot, she insisted again that no one but her should have been crowned queen, the highest honor possible at Saint Marie High.

"It wasn't fair," Christine continued, " and it wasn't right. The crown should have been mine."

"Ah, yes," Queen Julie rolled her eyes and took another drink herself. "I keep the tiara over my living room mantle in a hermetically sealed box. Getting crowned homecoming queen changed my life."

"Do you still have the crown?" Christine eagerly asked.

"No, silly, I gave it to the neighbor's child for a Halloween costume."

This angered Christine who claimed that one should show more respect for the homecoming queen's crown. She certainly would have.

"Losing to you was the most embarrassing moment of my life, worse than either one of my divorces," she cried angrily.

Enter the man to my left, who by this time couldn't resist, what with the metaphorical beating the former queen was taking at the hands of a mere princess.

"Oh, I don't know, Christine." He turned to her and smiled. "Remember that before the homecoming game, you had a fight with your boyfriend? And immediately after not wining the queen title, you disappeared off the stage and left your escort to drive the victory lap around the football field all alone in the convertible donated by Hansen Ford Trucks? "

"Oh my god." Christine's jaw crashed into the green beans.

"Did you wave?" asked the queen sympathetically.

"I don't remember," the man to my left's voice broke and he desolately poked his chicken. "I just remember driving around the football field all alone, abandoned. In front of hundreds of people."

"I remember that." Lisa said helpfully. "I remember feeling so sorry for you."

"OH my GOD." Christine, apparently still able to execute a few cheerleading moves, jumped on her chair to put even a bit of distance between herself and the man she wronged 20 years ago.

"He's kidding, right? " She pleaded from her perch, "he really doesn't remember after all these years?"

By this time I'm pretty impressed with my Miss Behaved husband. "The recovery therapy has helped him a lot," I supplied. "But he still wakes up every night crying, 'Christine, Christine, why did you abandon me?'"

"I think I was finally able to trust women again by the end of senior year, in college." He pulled in an impressive shuddering sigh. "It was just so traumatic for me. Possibly the worst experience of my life."

Christine's date, when he stopped laughing, coaxed her down from her chair but later refused to get in a car with her because he couldn't be sure she'd stay there. Lisa confided to me that Christine was kind of bitchy anyway and she, Lisa, was happy the man to my left brought up his experience.

The historian congratulated my husband for executing one the best-timed denouncements in the history of Saint Marie High School reunions.

I admired my husband for taking the Miss Behaved opportunity to sit right next to the person who did him wrong when he was 17.

I admired the homecoming queen for not even once raising her voice.

And I admired myself for never once admitting I was not a cheerleader and thus unqualified to listen to the private musings and public humiliation of the princesses.

Nope, it seems that being queen did not guarantee eternal happiness. Perhaps if she had kept the crown....

Dear Miss Behaved,

Every time I open a fashion magazine I get depressed. Why can't I lose five pounds? If I did, I'd be perfect and get a better job. I'm distracted and upset. I'm on a diet, but all I think about is food. Can you help me?

Signed,

Constantly in Need of Reassurance

Dear Constantly,

If you are becoming more and more depressed and upset that you do not, in any way, resemble the models in your favorite fashion magazine, the Miss Behaved advice for you is simple. Buy another magazine. *National Geographic* comes to mind.

A Better Boy Toy

◆

Dear Miss Behaved,

I overheard our receptionist say that her job wasn't the only thing in her life. "I am a wife and mother first," was her comment. This confused me because I didn't realize that being a wife was actually a job. I know that being a mother is a full-time job and I know that being the second wife is a job, what with recovering from surgical enhancements, spa visits, shopping sprees and all. But when did acquiring a husband mean that a woman has acquired yet another full-time project? This idea depresses me since I was considering getting a husband for myself, but not if he means more work. When did husbands gain the status of full-time job?

Signed,

Worried, But the Prospective Husband Is Pretty Cute

Dear Pretty,

Miss Behaved women everywhere were quite relieved to hear you ask this question out loud. It bears consideration because a generation of women exists who do not remember that popular TV shows once featured characters like a genie kept in a bottle who only emerged at her master's bidding, and that, for a few years, marriage was considered a career choice.

Years ago, during the second movement for women's rights, Gloria Steinem wrote a wonderfully Miss Behaved article on how she too would like to have a wife. But Ms Steinem stuck only to the basic jobs of a wife. We considered what it would be like not to have a wife, and certainly not to be the wife, but to be someone's full-time job. Wouldn't it be nice to acquire the ultimate Miss Behaved partner, who would perform the following tasks for little more than a pat on the head and free room and board (just like old-fashioned people claimed women worked for)?

The ultimate partner for the Miss Behaved woman:

- Has a cell phone. He is always on call and able to listen to her complaints about job stress and how easy he has it being home full-time.
- Is ready to meet for lunch or to create lunch or dinner for clients at a moment's notice.
- Cleans the toilets and does not expect great kudos for the effort.
- Times the dinner so it will be ready exactly when the Miss Behaved woman is ready to eat.
- Is a gourmet cook specializing in-low fat tasty dinners that are so good the Miss Behaved woman can barely tell that the meal is low-fat and good for her. (Because Miss Behaved eaters can always tell if someone is trying to slip them something of nutritional value.)
- Knows everything there is to know about wine and food pairings and carries maps of local wineries in the car just in case a spontaneous wine tasting is needed.
- Is a gifted shopper, willing to spend days at a time finding the perfect DKNY blouse at 50% off. Scours the outlet malls for a set of 350-count Egyptian cotton sheets for under $200. Discovers the perfect little store in Italy online that delivers double cold-press virgin oil within three days. Perfect for dipping his home-made bread.

- Has taken enough classes in decorating to be able to argue convincingly with the Miss Behaved partner that cerise on the living room wall is not a bad thing and who got an A in the decorating class anyway?
- Happens to be a certified masseuse and personal trainer. Also motivates the Miss Behaved woman to work out more and is knowledgeable in all sports so there is always a second to play doubles. Works out at the nearby gym so as to get many admiring looks which spur the Miss Behaved partner to greater achievement in her own muscle development.
- Has admirable stamina.
- Belongs to three book clubs and represents the Miss Behaved partner's opinions if she can't make the meeting because she's really slumming and isn't up for Isabel Allende and would rather just watch *Nash Bridges* on TV but loathes to admit it.
- Is able to convey very good gossip in a very entertaining manner, strictly for the Miss Behaved partner's amusement of course. Nothing personal.
- Never speaks of the Miss Behaved relationship in less than glowing, hearts-and-flowers terms. Relishes that others are jealous of the soul mate the partner has discovered.
- Every month, leaves a blue Tiffany's box at the breakfast table next to the freshly baked muffins and steaming Kona coffee.
- Grows and delivers the babies so the Miss Behaved stomach doesn't get all stretched and baggy.
- Has excellent parents, who are not annoying, live in another state, can afford to fly to where ever the Miss Behaved family happens to be for holidays, and they don't mind the wait at the airport during the high season.
- Knows excellent baby-sitters to take the children so the Miss Behaved woman and her partner can spend a romantic weekend away.

- Knows someone who knows someone who can get reservations at French Laundry for next October 12.
- Knows about gardening, so that all vegetables and tomatoes are fresh. Does not plant zucchini.
- Knows about landscaping and can be in charge of trouble shooting should a leak in the drip system cause a large fountain to squirt out from the center of the lawn.
- Mows the lawn weekly without being asked.
- Always takes out the garbage without complaining.
- Loves movies where the characters endlessly discuss theirs and everyone else's relationships. Is willing to pay good money to see a movie where they don't.
- Does not disappear into the garage for weeks at a time to "work on the car."

Fantasy aside, the question we'd like to ask Ms. Steinem today is, did you marry a husband or a wife? And does he ride a bike?

How to Get a Chain Saw

◆

This is the story of a husband who managed to acquire one of the most popular Miss Behaved tools for men: the chain saw.

It is best not to ask why a man who lives in the suburbs needs a chain saw. In fact for years the wife of this Miss Behaved fellow asked that very question, often quite loudly in the crowded aisles of Home Depot. At the time, the beleaguered male did not have an answer except that a chain makes a satisfactorily loud noise, is dangerous, and turns big pieces of wood into small pieces of wood. It would be a very practical tool but for the fact that the man's current home came equipped with two gas fireplaces.

Then the Miss Behaved husband attended his first lesbian poetry reading.

His attendance was not driven by an elaborate agenda well thought out ahead of time. It was more spontaneous than that. His wife was invited to read some of her work at a local and quite infamous venue close to his place of business. She accepted with alacrity. An audience is an audience. He (with the knowledge of most Northern California husbands) knew that, if he wanted to have sex any time during the next six months, he damn well better not only attend his wife's poetry reading, but smile about it. Anyone can do this for one night.

That evening, the nervous wife couldn't eat anything before the reading, so they planned (he graciously not mentioning he didn't have time for lunch that day either) on eating after her performance.

The reading was held at a tiny coffee shop that was not only had a reputation for supporting events that included poetry and interpretive dance, but also held the dubious honor for providing the slowest service in town. The Miss Behaved husband's office staff never ordered anything from this place unless there was a serious latte emergency and they had all afternoon. He knew better than to order anything. He'd have to pick it up the next morning.

Resigned, and remembering to smile at his wife every so often, our Miss Behaved hero sat at the far end of the tiny performance room, hunched down and concentrated on survival, as he was the only male within three hundred yards. He did recognize that, on the bright side, there would be no lines for the men's room. However, since there are never any lines for the men's room, this was not a compensatory feature of the evening.

For three hours, he suffered through four folk singers, three of whom came out of the closet that night and one of whom was still angry about something (he couldn't determine what). He listened to five poets each read four poems about growing old and wearing purple (best-case scenario), or walking the streets pushing a shopping cart (worst-case scenario), or staying young forever through random acts of immaturity like running naked through a lawn sprinkler at high noon. He heard one stand-up comic do a routine about roommates that was so bad he actually looked for an exit, but discovered they were all blocked by happy women with hair shorter than his own.

The Miss Behaved wife, to her credit, was aware of his hunger, his support, and the fact that he didn't dare express his true feelings toward the artistic works in progress. She also realized that not only was he the only straight man in the room, she was probably the only straight woman in the room. He pointed out that the attention paid to her was a good thing. She in turn pointed out that he was being fairly well-toler-ated and no one looked particularly angry that evening, for which he should be grateful.

During her own readings, she noted that the Miss Behaved husband made a concentrated effort to laugh in all the right places and even chuckled at an obscure reference to Henry Miller. As the evening waned, he became too delirious from hunger to realize that he ended up staying until the bitter end. His wife did sell two of her books, so she was quite happy and prepared to spend the cash treating him to dinner. But even as he was released, he discovered the bitter truth that a town that supports a coffee bar/lesbian performance art space is also a town with no restaurants open after 10:00 PM. The disappointed and hungry couple had to drive back to the suburbs and make due with the two remaining chicken pot pies in the freezer.

The next morning the Miss Behaved husband leapt out of bed and announced that this was the day he would purchase a chain saw. His wife's only possible response was an offer to drive him to Home Depot.

And that is how Miss Behaved husbands acquire power tools.

Cross Children Walk

Bad Birth Mothers

◆

Dear Miss Behaved,

I delivered my second child with nothing more than a few Popsicles and encouraging words like "don't push yet", which I ignored. My sister-in-law says that scheduled C-sections are the only way to go. My granola-eating mother thinks all drugs are bad. For me. Not her. What is the most Miss Behaved thing to do in this case?

Signed,

Flunked Lamaze

Dear Flunked,

Here are the Miss Behaved facts.

A recent article cites the alarming statistic that over 50 percent of birth mothers today use drugs to ease or completely eradicate pain during labor and childbirth. Experts are alarmed over this trend because in the early '80s only about 20 percent of birth mothers opted for pain medication during labor. Experts, doctors, and the people who rigorously defend their definition of contractions as 'a little cramping' profess to be quite concerned.

Birth mothers who use pain medication during childbirth are apparently being very Miss Behaved.

That is correct.

Miss Behaved birth mothers read up on medication options, they sign forms. They are armed with factual information about labor and childbirth that was presented to them during the baby shower while they were trapped between the clever hors d'oeuvres, (tiny hot dogs wrapped in a layer of phyllo dough), and the ice-cream punch, in colorful narrative complete with sound effects. The Miss Behaved mother-to-be observed the differences between the mothers who did and did not use pain medication during labor and decided for herself with which group she wished to associate. Often the Miss Behaved decision is based on who is wearing better shoes.

Miss Behaved birth mothers use every chemical in the book and stop anguishing about the process as soon as the baby arrives.

Miss Behaved Birth mothers know that, for them, the transformative power of pain will not lead to any kind of epiphany, but rather to twenty-four to thirty-six hours of unpleasantness. The natural experience of shrieking and beating the wall with whatever is handy—one's head, one's husband, a nearby nurse—is not going to make them a better person. In fact, lawsuits may be incurred during all the shouting.

Miss Behaved birth mothers are often older and more experienced in matters of control, delegation, and negotiation. Often they choose to delegate the pain to someone else. They choose to be comfortable. They demand services from hospitals, like a bed and an occasional Kleenex, damn the cost. They negotiate with their partners to 'participate' in the labor process, which, for the husband, often involves standing around the hospital room being yelled at. They are not wimps, these Miss Behaved mothers, they are strong enough to ask for what they want. In Miss Behaved tradition, they get it.

They watched the tapes in the mandatory Lamaze class. They were horrified.

The Miss Behaved question isn't why women are ditching natural childbirth. That is easily answered: because they are smart, conscious, and not easily influenced by sincere literature claiming this agony is the best thing to ever happen to a woman. Miss Behaved mothers are inclined to think that yes, certainly bringing life into this world is interesting and will alter their lives forever. But a Pulitzer would be nice as well, and just one trip to the Academy Awards would be just as memorable, and they would be better dressed.

The Miss Behaved question is why are these experts, these unnamed doctors, upset? Are they angry that women aren't suffering during this, the last great uncontrolled experience of a woman's life? Are the frightening stories of newborns, sluggish from the labor drugs and on the road to criminal activity, not working? Has the pain of labor actually been a deterrent to teen pregnancy? Will more women get pregnant because labor and birth is so 'easy'? Is it unfair that women have opportunities to run Fortune 500 companies and have comfortable labors? Do we have to pick just one?

This trend towards improving pain medication for women, improving the birth experience so that the mother isn't completely exhausted and beat up and can focus on her new baby, is marvelous. It could even be considered, in some circles, civilized and behaved.

If you are one of these doctors bent on punishment and pain, there are a few alternative Miss Behaved services we'd be happy to access for you. To Flunked Lamaze, we say, experience better living through chemicals.

The Miss Behaved Parent

$\blacklozenge$

Dear Miss Behaved,

My neighbors just allowed their children to drop out of both Little League and soccer. I have another neighbor who never signed his children up for anything in the first place. I know, without a doubt, that these parents are being terribly Miss Behaved I mean, what can they be thinking? How could these people not want to introduce their two-year-old to T-ball immediately? What about Tiny Tots Gymnastics? They could be part of our car pool for Tiny Tots and for soccer since the practices are held on alternative days. I don't understand why these slovenly parents deny their children the fun and team building of Pee Wee Football on Thursday, Friday, and Saturday afternoons; piano lessons first thing in the morning on Saturday, Monday, and Wednesday; and soccer practice on Monday, Tuesday, Wednesday, and Friday with away games every other Sunday afternoon. The character-building benefits of Girl Scouts on alternate Monday evenings and Urban Rangers on fourth and fifth Fridays of the month are incalculable. Don't these parents know that Good Parents need to enrich their children's lives by signing up and participating in sports and music? Don't they realize that in order for their child to even be considered for college, he must play four musical instruments, two of them well, be captain for three sports teams, MVP in two leagues, dance as the third snowflake in the annual Nutcracker, and be able to perform well on the PSAT with only three hours of sleep?

We just enrolled Lucinda and Zoë in horseback riding lessons, sailing, tennis camp, and golf, so when soccer and T-ball are over, the girls will have something to do.

My question is what decent American parent s wouldn't want all this opportunity for their child? Are my neighbors being Miss Behaved?

Signed,
The Perfect Parent

Dear Perfect,

Yes.

Not only are Miss Behaved parents denying their children all the fun and action that comes with spending five hours a day in the back of the family SUV, they allow their children to stay home after school. And, worse, Miss Behaved parents let their children watch TV.

Miss Behaved children are encouraged to sit still for an hour each day and watch Bugs Bunny, or something inventive on Cartoon Network. Miss Behaved parents approve of Nickelodeon for the children and the Comedy Channel for themselves. The shows Miss Behaved parents expose their children to are either entirely informative (Miss Behaved families know a great deal about sharks and crocodiles) or have no redeeming qualities what-so-ever, which is fine with the Miss Behaved parent.

Miss Behaved parents pay attention to commercials; they have favorites. The kids will call the Miss Behaved parents into the family room when their favorite commercial plays. The family sings commercial jingles in the car, eschewing camp songs (see Camp Sugar Cereal). They laugh because the songs make no sense at all. This is very Miss Behaved because conscientious parents know that every moment with a child should be instructive and informative.

Miss Behaved parents put the computer in the kitchen, even though everyone else has a computer in their own rooms. The Miss Behaved parents are not only interested in what the child comes up with during a search, they are also interested in what kind of games the children play on the computer. One Miss Behaved mother abandoned the boiling water for macaroni and cheese and listened to a full ten-minute explanation of Diablo II, during which she discovered that there are no mother characters in any video or computer game because no mother would let anyone run amuck with a sharp sword, let alone a flame thrower. There are no live mothers in Disney movies either.

One Miss Behaved mother allowed her child to read all the Harry Potter books in order over the course of a week in July. The child did nothing else and was even allowed to read at the dinner table and in the car. It is very Miss Behaved to spend a day with an uninterrupted read. Which is why Miss Behaved parents support it.

Another set of Miss Behaved parents take their oldest child fishing. They don't know why the child fishes; they shook the family tree but no explanation fell out. So, mystified but supportive, they drive the child to wherever he wants to go and they bring a book. The child sometimes doesn't catch anything, but happily spends three or four hours just sitting and casting.

Perfect Parents pass by the fishing lake on the way to the third soccer game of the afternoon and point out to their own exhausted children that this Miss Behaved child will never amount to much because he never learned to kick a ball. Everyone knows that kicking, hitting, and throwing are critical skills for success in high school, which leads to a good college, which leads to a good job that will pay for the SUV and soccer camp for the next generation.

This particular Miss Behaved family with the fishing child promised to let us know if the patience and perseverance their child is learning now does him any good later in life.

Miss Behaved children are allowed to clean the fish tank gravel in the bathroom sink, keep an African Pygmy hedgehog in the bedroom, and create a working model of a linear accelerator in the garage. The Miss

Behaved parent not only allows time for the child to pursue these hobbies, the parent is also willing to drive to the pet store to purchase another fifty pin-head crickets to feed the snake.

While Miss Behaved parents do not wish to spend twelve years worth of weekends driving the car from playing field to playing field, they are fond of long trips. As every good parent knows, family vacations that last longer than an overnight game in Ukiah are out of the question for the avid sports participant. No one leaves town during any season of any kind. Miss Behaved parents know this and they want no part of it. Why bother to become a grown-up if your schedule is still dictated by the requirements of the League B schedule?

Miss Behaved parents like to travel to common and exotic places and wish to pass on the spirit of adventure and discovery to their children. As much as football strategy is important, Miss Behaved parents feel that teaching the children to respect different cultures and negotiate rush hour traffic on the Underground may be longer-lasting skills.

At least if you're Miss Behaved they are.

What will become of the children of Miss Behaved parents? Who will be right? That's the real question: was purchasing the SUV, signing up for an intensive soccer seminar, dragging the child kicking and screaming to gymnastics for the entire fall season all worth it? For the sincere Puritan parents who (honest) only yell at the umpire, coach, and referee about twice a game, the answer is that for all this sacrifice, all this time away from the house, no life of their own, just driving in that luxurious tank of a car from parking lot to parking lot, the kid better not only learn to block defensively, he better amount to something.

When asked the same question the Miss Behaved parents answered that they didn't know as the children are their own people and will likely make their own independent decisions. But they sure have fun with the children right now.

Returnable Two

A Miss Behaved Cautionary Tale

◆

In the spirit of Jonathan Swift, Miss Behaved parents would like to point out that of the myriad of disasters that can befall a precious child, from falling from an 11-foot slide at daycare to eating sand, the one thing parents can be completely confident of, is the knowledge that their two-year-old child will never be kidnapped.

Consider those nasty and extraordinarily Miss Behaved custody battles in which each Miss Behaved party is simply out to injure the other equally Miss Behaved party. During the battle when it's time for that final desperate move when on aggrieved partner snatches a child and spirits it across international boarders all the while creating the script for the movie-of-the-week as they go, is that child ever 30 months? Or if a parent with a thirst for vengeance and retribution steals their flesh and blood from the other parent with a vague sense of retaliation, is the child toilet-trained?

Miss Behaved friends report that they themselves have passed up several boxes of two-year-olds labeled 'FREE' and placed in front of the exit door at Trader Joe's. Discerning parents finger the little darlings and mutter, "Hmm, she's a little damp and feels about 28 months. No thank you."

But, you protest, what about that kidnapping case involving terrorists and the Watermouth-Bellings of Impossible High Falls? That's right, there was one instance of a two-year-old kidnapped from the loving arms of two very Miss Behaved parents. Here is the Miss Behaved story.

The parents report that their darling two-year-old daughter, Lucinda Watermouth-Belling, was snatched from the back of their SUV at 8:00 AM on a Tuesday morning. The kidnapping wasn't reported until 12:00 PM because, frankly, Ms. Belling was so grateful for a silent ride to the daycare, she didn't bother looking behind her to see why the car was so quiet. Of course, once she realized that her child was missing, she took immediate action and dashed into Nordstrom to pick up the gray flannel slacks she had been eyeing but never tried on, because as soon as Lucinda enters a dressing room she instantly crawls under all the dressing room stalls, picks up twenty or so straight pins to play with, and escapes out the door to hide in the center of the round clothing racks for about an hour or so.

The kidnapping was reported immediately after the Watermouth-Bellings enjoyed a quiet lunch of grown-up food and rationally discussed their options. It was about then that the kidnappers, three renowned international terrorists, finally wrestled the cell phone away from Lucinda (she was dialing Big Bird to report that she rode in a car sans seat belt) and were able to call in their demands.

They wanted all the online codes to the Watermouth trust fund or little Lucinda would not be returned.

"Has she gone poop?" asked her father.

"What?" shouted the terrorist trying to hear over the Barney theme song that Lucinda was singing at the top of her lungs.

"Has she gone poop? Is she wearing her big-girl panties?" He turned to his wife, "Honey, do you remember if she was wearing her big-girl panties?"

"I think so, has she gone poop?" inquired the mother. She herself later admitted that at that very moment she was calling her manicurist to see if she could be fit in that afternoon. The last time she brought Lucinda to the salon, there were several incidents involving glass shelving, unbreakable bottles that weren't, and one or two minutes during which Lucinda escaped and Jennifer had to chase her down the street with wet nails and highlighting foil still in her hair.

"There was this mess," whined the hardened criminal, "and we cleaned her up but she won't wear what we found for her."

"You didn't go to Target, did you? They only have Pocahontas Underroos left and Lucinda will only wear the Teletubbies. Where are you? Maybe the Target there will have some Teletubbie Underoos left."

"We bought those diapers things," the terrorist admitted sheepishly.

"Now Lucinda knows those are only for nights and she has to try to use the toilet during the day. Put her on, we need to talk about this."

"Can we talk about the money?" pleaded the kidnapper.

"Have you fed her?"

"Yes." lied the kidnapper, to background noises of shrieks and falling bodies.

"She'll only eat the burgers out of McDonald happy meals," pointed out the calm father, picking at his own medallions of lamb and garlic potatoes. The last time they took Lucinda to a nice restaurant, she spent the bulk of the evening crawling through the planters looking for bugs.

"But I gave her a paper crown." protested the terrorist. "Then she opened all the ketchup packs. The car is a mess. There's a pickle on the roof and two of our anti-aircraft guns are jammed."

"She won't wear that crown, she only wears the Pretty, Pretty Princess crown, and only on alternate Tuesdays when there is tuna for lunch. No, has to be McDonalds. Otherwise she'll get cranky this afternoon and won't take her nap."

"You mean this is not cranky?"

"Hey, you're the experienced international terrorist. Call back when you've fed her. I'll be at the gym."

Two hours later the Watermouth-Billings received another call from the kidnappers with negotiations reversed. The Watermouth-Billings had to think about it, but decided that since Lucinda's grandmother was not only very fond of Lucinda, but also is the person who actually controlled the trust funds, it was probably worth the sacrifice. They took their child back.

Which is why the Watermouth-Billings now have the new Cadillac SUV, and Lucinda has two new sets of Teletubbie panties, two Pretty, Pretty Princess crowns, fourteen Happy Meal toys, and video copies of *Bugs Life* and *Tarzan* which she refused to watch quietly once the beleaguered terrorists dragged her back to the hideout.

Why are we reporting this Miss Behaved tale?

The Watermouth-Billings called to ask for Miss Behaved advice: should they go public with their story and risk glorifying kidnapping as an inexpensive form of baby-sitting? Or would a suggestion like that just inflame the self-righteous to protest that nothing is funny and the Watermouth-Billings ought to be more upset and further more ashamed of themselves for taking advantage of those poor terrorists who were just trying to do their job. And we certainly hope that the Terrorists represented a diversity of race and gender preference, otherwise this story would smack of non-inclusion and we can't have that.

The kidnappers themselves are not talking. They wish to preserve their hardened reputations and not spook their pending deal with Oliver Stone.

Miss Behaved wisdom predicts that in the film, Stone will use a small four-year-old.

Dear Miss Behaved,
What is the best kind of Miss Behaved swimsuit?
Signed,
Fifty Hours in Macy's So Far

Dear Searching,
The most Miss Behaved swimsuits are labeled 'Dry Clean Only'.

The NEA Grant Finalists

———————— ◆ ————————

Many Miss Behaved parents have asked this pertinent question: do the antics of their children qualify as performance art and, if so, is there a NEA grant?

Miss Behaved comparisons were made, including references to Karen Finley who once covered her nude body with chocolate and bean sprouts and danced around stage. One Miss Behaved parent couldn't recall what the point of the chocolate-bean-sprout performance was, (except there's always the sexual reference), but Finley's work didn't seem so very different from last Saturday's birthday party during which the birthday girl smeared herself with pink icing and glitter then ran screaming into the wading pool.

We heard tell of another ground-breaking performance artist who stood in a corner and whispered bad words as a renunciation of the societal restrictions placed upon our free expression. Many Miss Behaved parents claimed this work was derivative, as most recalcitrant three-year-olds do much the same kind of thing during their time-out on the day they discover the F word.

The Miss Behaved question is: can and should we call this kind of behavior art? Or should we just give everyone involved time-out and no cookies at snack time?

Since time-out doesn't necessarily pay, inspired Miss Behaved parents submitted summaries of the performances that were taking place all over the house. The Miss Behaved decision was if it gets a grant, its art. No grant, no cookies.

The Miss Behaved finalists
Fireplace Ash

This Miss Behaved artist scooped huge piles of soft ash from the fireplace in his fat baby hands and dumped the ash all over the white living room furniture and his smaller baby brother. The results were striking, the response from the sole member of the audience immediate.

Like any good art, the work inspired relevant questions: Was the baby brother a black version of Frosty the Snowman or a comment on race? Was it an expression of the dark days of winter, and how we all, occasionally, turn away from the sun? Was it a commentary on the futility of any mother presuming that there is a safe time to leave the children alone in order to use the bathroom in peace?

This piece, like all performance art, was transitory in nature and succumbed to vacuuming and a shower for all the performers involved.

Results: no cookie for the artist, two cookies for the screaming baby brother.

Watering the Stereo

One summer afternoon, this second Miss Behaved artist dragged the garden hose through the patio doors and proceeded to calmly soak down the TV and VCR. Offsite critics who only reviewed this art after the fact were interested in the subtext of the work. Was this an expression of the intrusion of the electronic media into our homes? Was it an overt and action-packed criticism of both the medium and the message? Did watering down the actual equipment add to the content quality of the programming *inside* the equipment?

The meaning of this work has been debated over many family Easter dinners, with the artist himself declaring that he was "just expressing himself," and felt "no negative feelings," from the results. His mother begs to differ and, after ten years, is still disinclined to give the artist any cookies.

Random Acts of Groceries

This piece is actually performed all over the country making it difficult to ascribe authorship.

Two Miss Behaved artists are required to create this piece. The first needs to be ambulatory since her job is to distract the parent by dancing in the aisles and commenting on the merits of toothpaste versus macaroni and cheese for dinner or of brushing one's teeth with the cheese paste from the macaroni box. The second child, who is conveniently placed in a back pack and thus behind the beleaguered parent, randomly lunges to the left or to the right and pulls down any product she can reach.

The final result is displayed at the checkout stand. While the first child triumphantly clutches her first tube of Aquafresh, the second child gloats over the predictable reaction of the parent who discovers that among the sensible purchases of milk and apples are three boxes of pectin, tie-dyed colored Fruit Roll Ups, a box of plastic glasses, kitchen matches, a glue gun, and seven boxes of Macaroni and Cheese in various promotional shapes.

If none of the items are brought home, it's art. If they are all brought home, it's defeat for the parent. Cookies for the artists, if they can sneak them out of the grocery bag during the ride home.

Holiday Dinner

One Miss Behaved artist expressed his support for the Indigent American People during what he feels has become a numbingly ritualistic and politically incorrect Thanksgiving Dinner. His protest in the name of the Native Americans manifested in the act of sliding off his seat, hiding under the table during the whole of dinner and refusing to eat anything but olives. The olives in question were carefully placed onto each round seventeen-month-old finger and bitten off carefully one-by-one. Some were shared with the dog, an innocent creature ignorant of the hypocrisy of the Pilgrims and subsequent historical myth-makers, and thus qualified to share in the olive bounty.

The artist believes that the fact that his parents were mortified by this piece is just another indication they are entrapped in the straight jacket of conformity, something he himself, as an artist, has so far been able to avoid.

The artist's grandmother, apparently not so tied to the appearance of things, later rewarded the artist with a small bit of pumpkin pie covered with a substantial amount of Cool Whip.

Not even Miss Behaved readers want to hear what the artist did when served a plateful of whipped cream topping, but a reference to Karen Finley would not be out of line.

Gifts from Miss Behaved Heart

◆

Dear Miss Behaved,

The holidays always exacerbate a fundamental problem with our family and I feel terrible for the children as a result of it. You see, I am still married to my first husband. We didn't realize how adversely our unusual relationship affected the children until yesterday when their friend Pete received many huge packages from his guilt-stricken father who wasn't particularly guilt-stricken when he abandoned the family to 'find himself' in the rain forest. But he's guilty now and it's easy to order off the net. Needless to say, we received 'the look' from our own children, and a running monologue about how great Pete's father is to send not one, but three new games along with the Sony Play Station IV.

Through tremendous self-control, we remained impassive to their admiration of the absent father. In fact, after the last state report during which my husband spent fifteen hours looking up exactly the right silhouettes of the state seal (a large rock) for the cover of the report on New Hampshire (the granite state), he feels the youngest child owes him. He has left many Home Depot catalogues around the living room, but to no avail.

How do I explain to the children that because we love them and love each other we aren't compelled to make it up to them in material goods?

Signed,

Still in Love for the First Time

Dear First Time,

It is remarkably Miss Behaved of you to still be with your first husband. Like owning season tickets to the ballet, you are being Miss Behaved just because the percentage of people doing such a thing is so terribly small.

But of course, since we are Miss Behaved, we have nothing but sympathy for your poor children. How terrible not to be able to contribute to the weekly conversations normal children share that involve house exchanges, convoluted travel schedules every weekend and step sibling foibles. To not be able to suggest solutions on how to determine where the favorite outfit is stored and which parent has the DSL and which does not (some enterprising children keep elaborate Excel spread sheets just to track where shoes are located). To not be able to brag about celebrating their birthday at a Six Flags amusement park because all *your* children got for their birthday was a homemade cake and a sleep-over.

As you are obviously aware, it's always worse at Christmas.

Children with intact families are at a distinct and obvious disadvantage during the holidays. Children living with happily married parents do not get to take a great trip to Aspen or Tahiti to meet the estranged parent who feels he/she may as well have a good time themselves while babysitting the kid. Truly fortunate children are blessed with disagreeing ex-parents. These ex-spouses are so concerned about turn-taking that they can't agree on which relative the child should visit during the holidays. What this means is that while the unhappy children of responsible parents must travel for five hours Christmas day to spend another six hours in Aunt Mona's overheated house and politely visit with Aunt Sheryl and Uncle Roger and not eat with his or her fingers (the child's, not Uncle Roger's) and smile continually, even if their gift is nothing more than a $25.00 savings bond, the child of the disagreeing parents is dropped off at the mall to spend *her* gift certificates at the Gap.

If this weren't enough, the children of divorced parents also have the guilt-bonus program thrown in which requires each gift to be bigger and better than the last. This includes the Christmas when a very large and expensive gift was required as a pre-emptive gesture to soften the blow of the remarriage announcement.

Miss Behaved pundits know that children of acrimoniously separated parents have the advantage of honing superior manipulation skills to pit one parent against the other (a skill that will serve them well later in life as they work through the jungle of corporate America). While the only thing the poor children of intact, original, families learn is cooperation, and that won't help a person in a Miss Behaved world at all.

So yes, you are right to feel badly. Your children are clearly at a disadvantage, not only in skill levels but also because you and your spouse not only talk and possibly agree between the two of you about the spending limits at Christmas, you are also committed to purchasing only those gifts that are appropriate. If you really want to rub it in, take time off from work and spend it with the children as a family. It may upset them at first, but they'll get used to it.

Compared to parents who know that when it comes to buying love there is no spending limit, you are being very Miss Behaved.

Camp Sugar Cereal

◆

Where can Miss Behaved children go for the summer? They do not want to hone new skills at tennis, horse or theater camp. They did download that Video Game Camp information and left it lying around the house for a while, but the Miss Behaved parents ignored it as it cost $2,000 a week. And by definition, Miss Behaved children are not fond of the traditional camp experience. They attended a traditional camp for one year, one of those programs that included an evening ritual during which sincere children sat around the fire and passed the talking stick. One Miss Behaved child expressed his inner feelings by bopping another child on the head. She was not encouraged to return.

What kind of alternative yet enriching experience can Miss Behaved parents secure for their children that does not cost trunk loads of cash or a Native American talking stick?

One Miss Behaved family was saved when they discovered Camp Sugar Cereal, a unique camping experience.

Since most camps have official camp shirts, the first thing the director of Camp Sugar Cereal did to prepare for camp was to order official camp shirts. In fact, this was the only thing the director did to prepare for camp. Thus the director (AKA Grandma) insisted that all campers and parents don the shirts immediately upon arrival and pose for the official camp photograph. Since this would also be the official Christmas card photo, everyone was required to smile happily. The clever director took the picture at the start of camp, before the Miss Behaved campers indulged themselves and wore those same shirts for three days and nights in a row until even the camp director noticed and found tongs to peel the offending garments off the campers' pungent bodies.

Outdoor Activities
Camp Sugar Cereal boasts that it provides a number of activities for the little Sugar Cereal camper. Many activities in the Camp Sugar repertoire are embarked upon only if the director is able to sit close by the activity site and read a book. To that end, each day of camp includes a trip to the director's good friend's pool. Pool activities include complimentary lemonade and looking up every minute-and-a-half to admire death-defying twists and jumps off the diving board.

Popular Camp Activities
A favorite activity at Camp Sugar Cereal is to watch television late into the night before the director realizes the campers are still awake. The director quickly learned that the campers were still awake and ventured upstairs every evening at about 11:00 to say firmly, "I don't think your mother would want you to watch that." To which the Miss Behaved campers guilelessly replied, "Oh of course she does, she just doesn't know it yet."

Then the campers explained to the director that the knife-wielding ax murderer in this particular movie is actually a profound metaphor for something and they'll know more if they are able to watch the film to its conclusion. But not even the Camp Sugar Cereal director is likely to fall for that one. But as part of the obligatory camp activities, the campers will try again the following night.

Failed Camp Activities

The Camp Sugar Cereal director claimed she suggested a hike or walk in the beautiful bucolic surrounds of Camp Sugar Cereal on many occasions. She was greeted with the typical response to the suggestion of outdoor exercise: both Miss Behaved campers fell down on the ground with mysterious cramping around the head, shoulders, and torso that would seemingly prevent them from any forced movement beyond painfully but successfully crawling to the television. At the beginning of the week-long camp, the director had enough energy to insist on a little walk and lured the campers into the car with the promise that fish, snakes, lizards, and a few dead animal carcasses would be discovered during their 'outing' (Never call it a hike). The director did have to check the instruction sheets to figure out how to disengage the Game Boys from the campers' hands.

Nutrition at Camp Sugar Cereal

True to its name, mealtime is when Camp Sugar Cereal truly shines and stands out from other camps in a significant way. No fruits or vegetables are killed during a Sugar Cereal meal. Breakfast selections include Cinnamon Toast Crunch, Rice Crispy Treats, Captain Crunch, and a donut or two. Often the campers eat their vitamin-fortified treats straight from the box while watching poorly animated Japanese cartoons. For lunch there is a tasty choice of corn dogs, microwave burritos, or more cereal. Dinner features such delicacies as macaroni and cheese or pizza. It is, in other words, a Miss Behaved child's paradise and one of the reasons Camp Sugar Cereal is so exclusive.

Camp Hygiene

At camp, the theory is that swimming in an over-chlorinated pool every day is a sufficient replacement for a real bath. This is supported by the camp director, who, you will recall, does not sleep on the same floor as the campers and simply insists they open the window in their room.

When the grateful parents retrieve the happy campers from Camp Sugar Cereal, they are fully prepared to place all the camp clothing into air-tight containers and drive the entire three-hour trip home with all the windows open.

The Sugar Cereal campers emerged from the experience unharmed and in fact, quite happy. They immediately showed off their new expanded vocabulary acquired on the afternoon the Camp director accidentally hit her thumb with a hammer.

The most important feature of Camp Sugar Cereal is something the average American child simply can't get enough of at home: benign neglect. Come and experience it at beautiful Camp Sugar Cereal.

Flour Babies

Teaching Miss Behaved Life Skills

◆

At our local junior high school, into every seventh grader's life a Flour Baby appears. A little bundle of joy, not from heaven but from science class. Flour babies are used as a hands-on tutorial to demonstrate to seventh graders what it is really like to care for a real baby 24/7 for just seven. One week. The Flour Baby my twelve-year-old cared for ended up being very Miss Behaved. We feel this came from the grandmother.

Friday afternoon: Enthusiastic twelve-year-old calls mother at work to remind her to purchase a five-pound bag of flour (nothing more, nothing less) and to ask if she knows where to get the flour? The Miss Behaved mother retorts that yes, she knows where to get the flour; she knows all about five-pound bags of flour and in fact didn't realize flour came in any larger amounts since a five pound bag of flour usually lasts about two years in her kitchen.

Later that same Friday afternoon: Mother picks up the bag of flour out of the baking aisle and discovers that this aisle also has shelves of bread mix and many different flavors of cake mixes. Well, who knew? Mother wishes, briefly, that picking out a real child was this simple.

Saturday: Twelve-year-old is delighted with new baby, immediately wraps the 'head' and 'bottom' of the baby in gray duct tape, explaining that this is okay to do but you can't wrap the whole baby as that would be silly, wrapping a whole baby in duct tape. The duct tape is supposed to keep the baby from leaking. Mother is not sure that teaching children to duct-tape babies is the best idea but does not comment since she doesn't want her Flour Baby to be the only one at school without duct tape. Peer pressure is a very real concern for Flour Babies.

Mother comments that her babies weighed in at seven pounds at birth, so the heavy lifting aspect of this project is not entirely accurate. Twelve-year-old patiently explains that some people were assigned a ten-pound bag of flour and another hapless friend was assigned twins.

Sunday afternoon: Mother suggests she take photos of the baby for the grandma album. Suggests taking pictures of the flour bag in the tub for "Baby's first bath", at the playground in the baby swing for "Baby's first trip to the park" and in the grocery cart for "Baby's first trip to the store."

Older sibling is mortified at the very idea and retreats to her room to call four friends. Twelve-year-old patiently explains that photographing the baby is not part of the assignment and didn't even make the top ten in the extra-credit list. And so, Mother can just stop the ludicrous suggestions.

Mother is resigned that this will not be as much fun as she hoped.

Monday morning: For Baby's first day at school, the Twelve-year-old borrows Mom's best hat to put on the duct-taped head. Laments that mother hasn't saved baby clothes. Mother points out that they needed to make room for the video game equipment.

Twelve-year-old pulls out contents of linen closet, rejects all the options, and leaves them in a pile in the middle of the living room floor. Defaults to his own pillowcase from his pillow. Finds a large safety pin. Wrestles with the large pin and the large amount of material while commenting that the teacher says that if they puncture the baby it's five points off.

Mother worries about Twelve-year-old puncturing self. Hopes there isn't the same system for real babies, as she would be working in large negative numbers by this time.

Tuesday night: For extra credit the Twelve-year-old needs to create a birth certificate for the baby. Flour Baby is a girl, named after mom.

Mother is flattered but wishes her namesake showed a little more spunk, but then it's difficult to read expressions under all that duct tape. On the birth certificate under 'State of' mother writes in 'shock'. Assures Twelve-year-old that the teacher will understand.

Wednesday morning: Twelve-year-old admits that Flour Baby moon-lighted as a football and was tossed back and forth during a game. Baby was dropped twice, but only on the grass. Twelve-year-old reports that the duct tape is holding up well.

Wednesday afternoon: Twelve-year-old is really tired of dragging the baby around during school, even if there is a 'nursery' in the science class. There are points off if you hurt another Flour Baby. Makes com-ments about baking Flour Baby into bread and claiming that the baby is just 'loafing around'. Mother wonders when this developmental stage will end, as it resembles the knock-knock-joke phase, in a bad way.

Thursday: Mother straps Flour Baby into the big plush baby seat attached to the Target shopping cart because they weren't invented yet when the mother had a baby this size and she wants to try one out. Twelve-year-old goes along with the madness for exactly seven sec-onds, then snatches Flour Baby out of the cart and abandons both the cart and the mother as quickly as possible by disappearing into the house wares aisle and forcing the mother to shop for hangers alone. It's not the same.

Friday: Child in tears, has forgotten baby on the bus ride home. By the time mother arrives home from work, the baby has seen more of the world than the Twelve-year-old. Mother visualizes calling the public transport lost-and-found and asking, "Have you found a five-pound sack of flour wearing a hat?" Decides to purchase a new baby instead. Tries to remember if it was unbleached and enriched or just enriched flour. Is pretty sure the duct tape will hide evidence.

Saturday: Twelve-year-old spends the night with friends. The child assures mother that the group will build a nursery for the flour babies.

Mother has secretly photographed Flour Baby by the side of the pool for "Baby's first swim".

Sunday: Mother picks up child from friend's house and sees that the nursery is a nice, dark, safe, area behind a bed. Mother hopes Flour Baby Protective Services are not around.

Twelve-year-old shares that another parent accidentally left a Flour Baby on top of the car and drove away. The ensuing explosion covered seven mail boxes with white flour. Everyone was quite impressed.

Monday afternoon: Apparently there is a peer ritual for the end of the Flour Baby session in which Flour Babies are hurled repeatedly into the school courtyard on their duct-taped heads. Mother is met with remains of Flour Baby in a zip lock bag tossed onto the kitchen counter.

All mother has left are the photographs. She is sorry she didn't get one of "Baby's last bus ride."

The Twelve year old in question has requested permanent anonymity and has hidden the photo album.

Middle Aged Woman on a Bicycle

◆

Dear Miss Behaved,

I'm in eighth grade and on the verge of joining only the most popular group in school. But all my dreams are coming to a total end because, like, my mother totally insists on going around town on, like, this bike! Why is she doing this? When there's a perfectly good car in the garage? It's not as if we don't have the money for gas or anything. How can I stop her?

Signed,
Desperate

Dear Desperate,

The bad news for you, and the good news for your parents, is that it is so easy for a parent to be Miss Behaved in the eyes of junior high girls. This is that special golden time when the parent can do nothing else but be Miss Behaved. All the parents have to do is get up, get dressed, and they are instantly being Miss Behaved. And if the goal is to be particularly Miss Behaved and really annoy your precious child, there is nothing so Miss Behaved as purchasing a new bicycle.

Did you accompany your mother when she bought her bike? Are you aware of what the equally Miss Behaved sales people recommended to your mother? They suggested something in pink, with a basket. Your Miss Behaved mother probably pointed out to you that the basket will be handy for books and papers so you can ride it to school when she's not using it. I know, imagine a thirteen-year-old girl on a bike, as if.

Your mother is also probably aware that in order to be completely Miss Behaved, the bike needs to have a bell or a horn on the handle bars. Equipped with a bell, she can ride the bike right up to the school, past the safety zone of the school parking lot (where the decent parents stay), ring the bell with a cheerful ding-a-ling and summon you from the playground where you are either cowering behind the dumpster or quickly disavowing any relationship to the aforementioned 'strange woman in the parking lot' to your friends.

But wait, it gets better. Your mother sounds like the prudent type. She will probably need a helmet. That's why you stopped riding a bike, yes? The helmet messed up your hair. Never mind, Miss Behaved women approve of big hair.

But your mother probably doesn't care about her hair. She probably thinks that a helmet is necessary for so-called safety reasons. The Miss Behaved news is that she will not only wear that mushroom-like hat during the bike ride, but might forget to take it off before walking into the schoolyard to hunt you down. Because by this time, you've escaped to the girls' bathroom and have told fourteen of your closest friends not, under any circumstance, to tell your mother where you're hiding.

The combination of bell, bike, and helmet should be so mortifying that you'll find it necessary to claim mental fatigue and stress and need to stay home for a couple of weeks. We know you're thinking that perhaps your mother will tire of her bike, or that it will rain. But don't bank your babysitting money on it. Miss Behaved mothers have the stamina to remain a long-term embarrassment to well-behaved and socially conscious daughters, often until the child can escape to college.

We feel your pain, but we can't help but congratulate your Miss Behaved mother on a job well done.

Graduation Awards

◆

Every school holds awards ceremonies to mark the accomplishments of the students. These award ceremonies are introduced at the preschool level, where the tiny graduates are dressed in ill-fitting robes, crooked mortar boards and forget to respond when their name is finally called. The ceremonies peak at high school graduation which now includes a mandatory party that only takes a year for the parents to plan and execute. A few children make it to college graduation where students don ill-fitting robes, can't get the mortar boards straight, and forget to respond when their name is finally called.

Which is all very well and good for the child. But what about the parents of all those successful children? Miss Behaved people often watch these elaborate award ceremonies and wonder, did the child do this work all by herself? Did that scholarship just fall into his lap while he was playing Ogres Dance for N64?

We think not. Miss Behaved people know there is always more to the story. Miss Behaved people also expect to be rewarded for any effort great or small. We think there should be parent awards slipped in between all the recognition the kids receive, if only for a very brief reality check.

The Miss Behaved Parent Awards

Best Use of a Glue Gun

Cindy Harrison received a seventh-grade certificate for straight As this semester.

Her mother, who worked with Cindy every evening on that large medieval castle project with a working moat, sacrificing her time, her energy, her own work, and the finish on the kitchen table, received a box of Godiva Chocolates in the shape of tiny Crusade shields.

Best Driving While Under the Influence of Cold Medicine

Pete Callihan received a trophy for perfect attendance for soccer.

His father, who drove to each and every game rain or shine, even when he had a bad case of the swine flu which rendered him incapable of driving to work but still able to deliver four children to five different locations during the second worst storm of the season, received a new cordless drill with a selection of ten bit sizes, two of which he didn't already have.

Best Feigned Interest While Listening to Another Plot Summary of *Party of Five*

Susie Meyer, the last of the five Meyer children, received a high school diploma and a trip to South America to study birds for a year.

Her parents, Lisa and Jack, were awarded with an empty nest and the freedom to not appreciate the finer musical points of Stain.

Best Interpretive Dance Illustrating a Hyperbolic Curve

Cindy Okanawa received special recognition for overcoming her learning disabilities and graduating from high school with honors. What a brave girl!

Her parents, Stephanie and Mike, who took turns every night for 12 years to help Cindy through every blessed homework assignment as if they really wanted to learn yet another way to do algebra (and there was that week that Mike threw out his back because he acted out all the parts to *As You Like It* so Cindy would understand enough to write her 8-page paper), received a free consultation with a chiropractor.

Best Use of Acronyms

George Richards received an award for Most Improved during his eighth-grade year.

His mother, who clocked in the longest IAP meeting on record, at three hours and thirteen minutes, as she explained to the current RSP, IAP, PSI, URL and ASP specialists all the results from the last seven years of RSP, IAP, PSI, URL and ASP evaluations, to make certain that they would understand, specifically, what George's needs were and how best to instruct him, received a massage.

Best Reason to Take up Daily Jogging

Ben Foo received a scholarship to UOP to play in the university orchestra.

His parents, Margaret and Tony, who endured ten years of violin practice before Ben learned to subdue the high notes and not make the dog howl with each practice, and there was that one afternoon the animal protection league came to the house on suspicion that someone was brutally torturing a Chihuahua, received accupressure therapy for their hearing.

And then there are those special Miss Behaved moments of parenting, the acts of intuition and faith that, at the time, the receiving party resents like hell. However, in the long run, these decisions have their own rewards. Parents know this.

To Greg and Jennifer Silvers, who bit their tongues when their only daughter began dating the most inappropriate boy in the school, with no family background to speak of, so of course they fell in love and dated exclusively through high school, and were voted 'Cutest Couple' in the yearbook and looked perfect together at the prom and he proposed on the dance floor (which was very romantic), and promised he could get a good job installing car stereos at 'Noise 4 U' and she could work at Rite Aid, the announcement in June that Shanna, the light of their life, is breaking up with Mr.Car Stereo and will be attending Stanford in the fall.

To the Franklins who refused to allow their high school sons to attend spring break in Florida and so had to sit through an excruciating week of the boys watching endless clips of the aforementioned spring break festivities on MTV while pointing out morosely that it should be them on the beach with the babes instead of them staying home alone in this god-forsaken, snow-covered, homestead, the phone call from a family friend who told the Franklins that seventeen young men were rushed to the emergency room after one too many beer bongs, three of whom were the close friends of the cranky, stay-at-home teens, the expression on their darlings' faces when they said, "We told you so."

To the Petersons, who did not give the car keys to the twins that night of the five-car-pile up on highway 12, nothing.

Travelers Tales
Out of Turn

Las Vegas

*Which is Miss Behaved all by itself
and needs no additional help.*

◆

It is difficult to be Miss Behaved in Las Vegas and have anyone notice. For instance, if there is a full-scale cannon battle between a pirate ship and a British ship raging in front of your hotel with men falling off the rigging and large objects bursting into flames that can be seen for a mile or so down the strip, pulling the fire alarm seems a bit paltry.

If Las Vegas doesn't need any Miss Behaved help, why go there? Shouldn't a Miss Behaved tourist be doing his part to upset the delicate balance of tourism in other parts of the country by dragging his sticky children to antique shops in Vermont? Well, of course, but Las Vegas has unique Miss Behaved charms that are not to be missed.

In Las Vegas a Miss Behaved tourist can blend right in. One can relax in surroundings created by marvelously Miss Behaved developers and planners whose sole purpose is to keep you, the Miss Behaved tourist, where you are. To entice you spend all your money in the first hotel/casino you enter.

Here, also, a tourist can purchase any and every item imaginable from a Hermes scarf ($275) to a size XXL pink Flamingo Hotel sweatshirt ($274). Ashtrays sporting the hotel logos are sold everywhere, because, here, in the land of the Miss Behaved, people can smoke indoors.

In fact, because Las Vegas represents one big Miss Behaved vision, many Miss Behaved tourists consider the town their own Miss Behaved Mecca.

Seven Miss Behaved reasons to love Las Vegas:

First: it's very Miss Behaved to build a large-scale piece of civilization in the middle of the desert. How many cultures have thrived with no water? Not many, even fewer cultures build casinos.

Second: the men who invented Las Vegas were Miss Behaved in truly profound ways, and since this is America they flourished much like the imported tropical plants nourished with all that redirected water which surround the Mirage.

Third: Vegas is all about bright lights and shiny things. Vegas is all about distraction and illusion. Some claim that Las Vegas is all hustle and the change over from Mafia control to corporate control hasn't altered the goals, reality, or enforcement techniques of the place one tiny bit. They are right. And no one cares. As any hard working Miss Behaved Marketing Executive will tell you: it's not hustle; its astute brand management.

Fourth: the Miss Behaved activities are perfectly balanced in Las Vegas. It is the only city in the world where one can find husbands happily trailing their wives as the women claw through the racks at Saks. The Miss Behaved husband knows that, for once, patience in the department store will be reciprocally rewarded later with an evening devoted to drinking, gaming, and ogling professional breasts.

Fifth: everyone stays out past bedtime. The streets are packed with people who are not eating enough fiber and not getting their required eight hours of sleep. Apparently nothing bad is happening to them, save a few major losses at the blackjack table.

Sixth: you can touch everything (except the professional breasts). As many Miss Behaved shoppers know, if one is wandering around Union Square, or Rodeo Drive, or Fifth Avenue, one is not even remotely encouraged to storm the gates of Gucci just so one can stupidly ask the price of those handbags. But in Las Vegas, there are no gates, no door monitors. A Miss Behaved shopper can not only walk into any upscale store and touch anything in the cases, she can ask for prices. The salespeople comply because they cannot tell from your demeanor or your outfit if you just won at the tables, if you are one of the last wealthy dot-com slobs, or if you are just eccentric. If you've harbored Miss Behaved fantasies of running your grubby hands through Hermes silk or Versace sequins, this is your town.

Seventh: Las Vegas changes with the times. One Miss Behaved tourist recalls his first experience of Las Vegas back in the seventies. As his parents drove down Fremont Street, he could see inside the casinos. The entrances were a block long, open to the sidewalks and the hot desert air. Even in the middle of the night, the sidewalks teemed with people. The decorative facades of the casinos and hotels bulged out over the street and flashed bright yellow, gold, and pink neon against the black desert sky. A towering neon cowboy dominated the street and waved to the crowd below.

His parents explained that Las Vegas existed solely to lure people into losing lots and lots of money and sometimes their virginity. Many lectures from the front of the car on the evils of gambling ensued as the family car crept down the length of the strip. Las Vegas, he was told, was Sin City. He could hardly wait to come back.

When he did return, he discovered that the luxury hotels on the new strip are not covered with flashing neon and running lights; they are much classier than that. Huge video screens dominate the new strip and continuously play commercials for their shows, rooms, and Starbucks. Green light periodically washes over the faux front of the Venetian. The volcano fountain in front of the Mirage erupts on schedule with flames, smoke, and red lights. Las Vegas is almost indistinguishable from Disneyland with the minor additions of alcohol, gambling, and naked breasts.

With the last feature in mind, our Miss Behaved tourist headed to the famous Paradise Palace. This is the most popular topless club in Vegas mostly because the floors aren't sticky.

The dancers in this topless club, or the topless women in this dance club, are perfectly Miss Behaved. But they are not Miss Behaved merely because they take their tops off for money, although stripping ranks with rocket scientist on the top Miss Behaved career list (but only if you're a girl, in fact for both of these jobs it's better to be a girl). Nor are strippers or exotic dancers Miss Behaved because they manage to wear thongs without clutching themselves every thirteen minutes. Nor are they Miss Behaved because they can dance, climb stairs, and stand upright for five minutes at a time while wearing six-inch platform shoes (an admirable skill but non-transferable).

These ladies are Miss Behaved because they are so damn bored.

Our Miss Behaved tourist reported watching a lap dance performed by a young lady, who while executing the value-priced lap dance, only $40 for ten minutes, got an eyelash in her eye. So she turned her back to the customer, whose own eyes were closed in either bliss or drunken stupor, and worked the eyelash out of her eye while automatically bumping and grinding. Mostly grinding.

Another Miss Behaved guest admired the methodology of the girls. She liked the way the dancers first advertised their skills with a tabletop dance, during which men tucked money into the dancer's thongs or just threw bills onto the table. When the preview ended, the girls stepped off the tiny stage and circulated around the floor in order to solicit a more private dance at a higher price. The solicitation is as perfunctory as a long-distance-carrier telephone solicitation. If you refuse a dance, they quickly move on—no cash from you, no smiles from them.

Miss Behaved information has it that dancers at a club like this can pick up about $2,000 over the weekend if they're any good at all. Some dancers are college students (we know what you're thinking; but this is a job for the very young, it is better not to have used any of your parts) in California or Nevada who fly out and work one weekend a month. This is one of the best Miss Behaved ways to make money—be young, take off your top, and happy men throw money at you. What could be easier?

We think this is a much better program than Mardi Gras because when a girl takes off her top there, all she gets is beads. And what can a girl buy with 75 pounds of plastic beads?

A Miss Behaved Drive in the Country
Or Where We Spent Our Summer Vacation

◆

For our summer vacation we wanted to make our lives easy, so instead of taking an elaborate or dangerous trip such as white-water rafting or spelunking, we simply took relaxing drives in the country. The country in question was England. We took my mother.

We began the drive through England's Cotswolds district because the Cotswolds are the prettiest part of England and my mother, in charge of the trip and the maps, decided we didn't need to waste time looking at the ugly parts.

My husband was named the designated driver as he had the lowest blood pressure. At least he did at the start of the trip.

My mother was the designated map reader. This meant that every fourth mile or so she'd pull off her glasses, squint at page 92 of the three-foot-square atlas and say, "Now the B-4580 will get you there directly but if you take this smaller white line, the C-2049, and connect with the red line which is, wait, the D-6978, it looks like we'll avoid the M4 completely. If you take the D-3904 which is coming up on the right, it will lead to Chippingtoast Manor, which is very interesting but we don't want to go there."

As we sped through one picturesque village that, while lovely, apparently held nothing of any real interest, we approached a lovely ancient bridge decorated with a sign that noted "On Coming Traffic Down the Middle," which meant that the road under the bridge is only big enough for one-way traffic. It also meant that the large blue Mercedes diesel truck bearing down on us, trapped in the tiny rental car that Mom claimed was the largest in the fleet, was suppose to, in theory, yield the right away to us. But since the truck was already halfway through the tunnel and we weren't, we didn't challenge the semantics of the sign. I'm sure this tunnel was historic but we were all too terrified to focus on the fine pediment work.

Our two children, survival instincts evolving to a new level, crouched in the back seat and studiously played with their Game Boys. Occasionally they glanced up and pointed at a cow.

The most important skill my husband acquired while driving in the country was how to get in and out of the round-abouts without causing undue stress to my mother. The trick to negotiating these alternatives to four-way stops is learning to read the round-about signs which resemble aboriginal cave art and determine which arm off the primitive sun painting you want. One can only pause at the entrance to the round-about for a moment before fearlessly plunging into the circle while remembering that the cars already spinning around have the right away. With luck and some centrifugal force, the car will circle a half dozen times and fling out towards the correct direction which is heading towards Mangotsfield, but we don't want to go there—we want to get off before that onto the E-9540.

We purchased our first tank of gas in Bourbon-on-Water. As the tiny car gulped liters of gas running at roughly $10 a gulp (US), my husband and I stood to one side and did our Lamaze breathing. It was a worthless skill during the birth of our children but very effective for calming down enough to reach for the credit card and hope the limit holds long enough to cover the price of petrol. Bridges, hedgerows, and tunnels aside, gasoline prices are the main reason there are no large cars in the country, a natural selection process that Americans would do well to look into.

Nope, we're too spoiled.

Since driving up to this point had only produced a half dozen adrenaline rushes, including an encounter with a hedge-trimmer and a close call with a duck, my husband decided to end his country driving with a final drive down the M4 and straight into London.

"Oh no," my mother protested, "you can't drive into London. We'll take the train."

"Oh no," protested the innkeeper, "we never drive to London; we always take the bus."

With gas prices what they are, one could hire a helicopter and come out ahead.

My mother's plan for getting to London included driving for three hours in the opposite direction in order to leave the rental car in a city with a name that beings with O. I don't remember which one. We would then take a train that leaves from there to London three times a day and she hopes we won't miss the mid-day departure. From the train station it's seven stops on the Underground. Then a four-block walk to the hotel with each person taking a turn carrying the suitcase that holds the stone gorgon's head purchased at the beginning of the trip in Bath. My husband, who has always wanted to experience the thrill of bungee jumping, but could never find the time, decided that driving the M4 sounded like a sufficient substitute. We drove into London.

The M4 was like any other freeway and included, as a bonus, clearly marked signs that matched points on the large-scale map I was in charge of because Mom was too tense to direct. In fact, she put me in charge of directing the driver to the hotel, clearly marked on page 198 of the London A-Z book. Unfortunately, unlike my mother, I did not attend the seminar on how to read the London A-Z book. A thick black line depicts every road, every street is an equally thick line, and as I flipped from page to page it seems that east and west are not consistently depicted and I have to turn the book clockwise as we progress down the street. Despite my mother's insistent claims from the back seat that the hotel was clearly marked, I could not find it. The hotel—I apparently had the map in my hand.

While traffic zipped around us and stop lights blinked and my son evolved his 97th Pokemon to the next level, my exasperated mother finally snatched the book from my hands and said, "It's right there. I don't know how you could miss it".

She had made a small ink dot marking our destination; the ink dot was one in a sea of twisted lines and dots on the map. If I were a child skilled in finding and picking even the smallest sliver of onion out of my spaghetti sauce, I would have found that dot easily enough. But I'm not and I didn't.

With more luck than skill, we found the hotel. My husband paused long enough to dump the luggage onto the sidewalk and tersely instructed the kids to take care of their grandmother. We sped away to return the rental car in solitary splendor, a new map (provided by the rental company with their logo and a yellow arrow pointing to our new destination) in our hands. As we walked slowly back to the hotel, we felt that our transportation challenges were over, since London is famous for its extensive subway system and we planned to take the tube because it, like our credit cards, was everywhere we wanted to be.

What we did not realize was that the Underground stop for our hotel was only accessible from the Earl's Court exchange, because the other route on the Circle Line was closed due to repairs. We were obliged to always travel through the Earl's Court which was what every other tube passenger in London was doing. No one knew where they were going because every other train coming in from the right seemed to be traveling east, and every third train was traveling west. During the three seconds the train paused and the crowd surged into the cars, the sign designating where the train was really heading east, west and on two occasions, south, changed just as the doors closed. Mind the gap. We spent one afternoon traveling east, then west, then east again, wondering finally if we just couldn't get there from here. The children wondered out loud if Grandma and her directions weren't the better bet.

But we had plenty of time to admire the Underground maps at each station. They were all clearly marked.

The Gift Store Tour

◆

It was the gift shop attached to the sod house out in the middle of the prairie in South Dakota selling chunks of well, sod, that inspired me to gather information on adventures in retail. For the Miss Behaved traveler, the whole point of a trip, even if it's down the street, is to acquire more stuff. There wouldn't be a gift shop attached to the car wash if we weren't meant to purchase something. Acquisition is not only very Miss Behaved, but practiced so widely and consistently that it is often the foundation for entire economies. Miss Behaved tourists like nothing better than to spend precious daylight hours wedged into state-owned gift stores seriously sorting through *Inspired by native art* magnets.

There are rules to be followed before a Miss Behaved souvenir is purchased.

First, it must be completely impractical and useless even as a doorstop, like a chunk of sod.

Second, it must be easy to get. Consider the popular Aloha shirt. It is seen as a happy tribute to warmer climates and the uniform of Miss Behaved brotherhood when worn on the mainland (except on the west coast, where business people own a dozen Aloha shirts and wear them to meetings with venture capitalists). It often comes from the heavily advertised Hilo Hatties. This store sends busses out ten times a day to canvas the island. Tourists are gathered and brought back to the Hilo Hatties warehouse that is filled with so much brightly colored clothing that the tourists immediately fall into a stupor. They awake only after they have acquired His and Hers matching Aloha shirt and muumuu because (and this is the essence of the Miss Behaved souvenir) it seemed like such a good idea at the time.

Third, a souvenir must be difficult to bring home. One Miss Behaved tourist reports that he was so swept up in the moment, he used his last half-dozen traveler's checks to purchase a fabulous hand-carved surfboard from Bora Bora that was so fragile it could only be transported via carry-on. He lost many friends on the flight home. The subsequent reaction of his wife when he suggested that the surfboard would look great over the fireplace and could replace the largish portrait of the children, a gift from her mother, was very Miss Behaved.

Most Miss Behaved travelers know that museum gift stores are the best excuse for purchases because they offer the patina of education. This attitude helps encourage and nurture overwhelming impulses to purchase items like a working telescope for the oldest child because she actually paused at the 'Expanding Galaxy' exhibit and only whined twice that she was hungry, thirsty, and tired.

Aside from chartered busses and educational stores (one Miss Behaved family has yet to admit that the glow sticks and key chains purchased from the Discovery Museum Store may not actually possess educational value, but it seemed a good idea at the time), the favorite kind of gift shop are the Disney-inspired shops strategically positioned at the exit of every point of interest in the world, from the Mystery Spot to the Tower of London.

One Miss Behaved tourist shared that her family managed to spend more time in these gift shops than they did actually admiring the tourist attraction in question. Remember, it doesn't matter if you liked the trip, only that you picked up a significant item every time you stopped the rental car or got off the bus. Our Miss Behaved tourist doesn't remember when it happened, but at some point she realized that the family historical trip through England's past had narrowed to the Gift Shop

Tour of Britain.

This Miss Behaved Gift Shop Tour began at the Falconry in the English Cotswolds. The Falconry was a tiny showplace that in no way resembled Sea World since it was about birds. The youngest child craved a stuffed owl with realistic eyes, but that was vetoed in favor of five key chains and a set of laminated walking maps of the Cotswolds even though the family was leaving the next day.

The mystical, mysterious, awesome Stonehenge is fronted by a very nice gift shop with disappointingly tasteful offerings. No Stonehenge bracelets or necklaces with jangling stones that could be added on to the chain at each Solstice. No Stonehenge building blocks (Make your own! Finish the circle and align it with the sun and moon!). But the Miss Behaved traveler persevered and purchased a parachute-sized scarf decorated with the circle of stones colored in pink because that's prettier. After recovering from the lack of Aloha shirts, the family defaulted to buying the official Stonehenge chocolates, which, at the time, were absolutely essential. The chocolate melted into the scarf because both ended up at the bottom of the backpack that ended up at the bottom of the car floor next to the heater that only worked for an hour which was also the same hour the sun finally broke through the persistent overcast. It happened on Tuesday at 1:00 PM EST.

The Jane Austen museum in Bath was a bit sparse, since it just opened. There were a couple of authentic items in the main museum, but most of the Jane Austen stuff was located in the gift shop. The stuff consisted of reproductions of other stuff, mugs, and of course, her books. The Miss Behaved female tourists (the men stayed outside with sudden headaches) enjoyed the tour of the tiny museum and of course purchased three mugs inscribed with witty Austen quotes, paper dolls and a half dozen postcards. The Miss Behaved justification was that if every visitor spent a bit of cash, the tiny museum could stay open.

The Roman Bath Museum offered an array of important gift items in its extensive and crowded shop, not the least of which was a marvelous gorgon's head carved in stone. It weighed 25 pounds, and thus the perfect purchase with which to begin a long trip that would involve many train changes and carrying luggage for blocks and blocks in the unexpected heat of the afternoon. The gorgon head only got a little chocolate on it. It was easily rinsed, and left only a slight nick in the hotel sink.

After spending the morning touring the only coal mine in Wales open to tourists. And after slipping and sliding on the damp slag and watching the Miss Behaved children purposely hit their heads on low wood beams because they got to wear hard hats for the first time, anything in the light of day looked good. At the Coal Mine gift shop, the Miss Behaved husband purchased a photo book of the world's best mine explosions, four pieces of licorice that looked like genuine coal, and a CD of Welsh songs performed by former coal miners. For parties.

Contrary to popular Miss Behaved wishes, Stratford-upon-Avon bore no resemblance to the Renaissance Fair, or even to Ashland. But between each place of birth, resting-place, sleeping-place, death-place, or drinking-place of Shakespeare, lie ten gift stores of various tastes and themes. Even our Miss Behaved tourists passed on the busts of the Bard (no sign of Ben Johnson) and they saw *Shakespeare in Love* on the plane but were not compelled to purchase their own copy. But the miniature knights in shining armor were a must-have, as was a small working cannon. We know, but the Queen Elizabeth Dolls weren't appealing to anyone, no matter how scary.

One of the most convenient ways to be Miss Behaved and give a sense of purpose to the shopping experience is to begin a collection: Knives of the World, Firearms of the Wild West, Heavy Objects That Must Be Shipped. Any group of things that have to be explained item by item to every guest who haplessly wanders into the display room (other wise known as the formal living room) is appropriate. One Miss Behaved tourist collects thimbles painted with tiny pictures of national monuments even though he doesn't sew. Another Miss Behaved tourist collects coffee spoons even though she doesn't drink coffee nor plans to use them to measure out her life.

But gift shops, for all their appeal, raise an important Miss Behaved question: is there a difference between a pink coated souvenir wine glass with a gold logo of the Winchester Mystery House and a souvenir mug with a Jane Austen quote? Is the more obscure and difficult-to-find item (the surfboard comes to mind) somehow more classy because it's harder to get? Or is any purchase made while traveling legitimate and worthy of third-party admiration because it was acquired with a dash of irony and resulted in lasting credit-card debt? Even Miss Behaved tourists concede that this line is as fuzzy as dice from the carnival and as difficult to draw as the difference between placing pink flamingos on the lawn because it's ironic or because the pink plastic compliments the plaster dwarf family already in place.

Obviously one has to look for the dwarfs to be sure.

They can be purchased at Ye Olde Curiosity Shoppe in Dublin, with outlets in Solvang California, Old Town Sacramento, Disney World, and Wall Drug.

Dear Miss Behaved,

I'm tired of my husband; he never hangs the toilet paper the way it should hang. Should we divorce?

Signed,

Fed Up

Dear Fed,

When women grow tired of their marriage partners, there are a few Miss Behaved methods for quickly improving the situation without resorting to divorce. We have noticed that one of the biggest Miss Behaved problems with divorce is that, like when you were children, you have to divide all your stuff equally and share. Some couples end up sharing more post marriage than they did during the marriage. To protect your assets, we have a Miss Behaved suggestion.

Before you divorce, trade husbands with another disgruntled friend. Like borrowing someone's dress for a party or trading recipes, this Miss Behaved solution has the advantage of being cheap and brief. After a week, most wives (and perhaps husbands) will make the Miss Behaved discovery that most marriages are depressingly similar. What one husband does well will be countered by something he does that is murderously annoying. Commit to the exchange for no longer than one week; most husbands are returned in a matter of days.

Miss Behaved in the Great Outdoors

———————————— ◆ ————————————

Dear Miss Behaved,

My husband wants to go camping. This is our first family trip and all of the information and advice about camping has been gleaned from the Internet. My husband's own parents rarely ventured outdoors except to travel down the driveway to pick up the daily *Wall Street Journal.* He claims this will be a family adventure and bring us all closer together and I agree. We own one two-person tent and have three children.

I am worried this adventure will resemble the east side of the Survivor Island where people eat rats under supervised conditions. I want the experience to be like the opposite side of the island where the television crew enjoyed using ping-pong tables; slept in temperature controlled RV's, and ate catered food. My husband assures me he will not make us eat rats because the rats.com site assures that there are no rats where we are going. I do not find this comforting. Apparently there will be no cash prizes at the conclusion of our adventure.

Two of the choices my husband has presented so far are tent-camping and car-camping. If we tent camp we must carry out all our garbage back to the car which I think is too yucky to contemplate. Car-camping however involves staying at some place like KOA Land O' Cement where we will spend a week in the bucolic outskirts of some suburban outpost stuck next to people who play the stereo too loudly and sing *1,000 Bottles of Beer* well into the next morning. I worry about the children getting run over at the campsite by people driving to each other's double-wide RV.

My husband then reassured me that he is not interested in car-camping because the point of this exercise is to explore the great outdoors, not stay close to civilization. I will add that he glossed over the garbage-carrying part as unimportant and swears that I will be so thrilled with the scenery and splendid isolation of the experience I will not notice the coffee grounds dripping from my backpack.

To explore this great isolated wilderness we need a canoe. His current plan is for us to carry the unwieldy seven-foot thing eight miles into the woods to Lake Clear and Cold. He claims he has read reviews from several web sites that it is not only wonderful to have a canoe but we can dive off the side into the glacier-fed water and bathe.

This raised the question of facilities of which I discovered there are none. My husband claims that according to three out of five web sites, the point of camping is to get in touch with nature. If this is true, I fear that by the end of the first day I will have come into contact with considerably more nature than I ever have in the past and I'm still not entirely clear on what poison oak looks like.

Once I recovered from the cost of the canoe, I noticed that my husband had acquired many, many items from CompleteOutDoor Man.com. These necessary camping items include five extra-fluffy down sleeping bags, four pairs of fully waterproof boots, jackets, hats and gloves all made out of Gore-Tex, ice-cutting tools, and a new graphite fishing pole. I realize my own experience is limited, but I assume these are not the cheerful harbingers of a trip that includes sunbathing.

I asked, but there will be no Sherpas, no guides, and no porters to carry the bags or the canoe.

I have deep concerns about coming in contact with poison ivy hanging from trees, fierce sea lions, and eyelash vipers.

I'm worried that my new hiking boots will not only hurt but also ruin my feet for pumps.

According to the handout my second youngest brought home from the American Lung Association, secondhand smoke is deadly. Statistically, campfire smoke must count. Not only that, the residue from burned marshmallows probably creates a sticky substance that will coat the fragile alveolus in my lungs and create permanent damage.

And when was it decided that outdoor cooking is superior to room service? You can order hot dogs burned on the outside and cold on the inside, the people at the Four Seasons are very accommodating.

I've heard friends explain they 'wash' their pots and pans out with sand. Revisiting the getting-in-touch-with-the-outdoors-situation, I feel that doses of sand with the food will probably aggravate the situation. And who is carrying the pots and pans in the first place? I had to remind my husband that the Calphalon Professional Series is very heavy.

If a fish is caught does that mean we need to eat it, or can I claim that it's ecologically unsound to pull the fish from its natural ecosystem and I brought a frozen pizza anyway, so the fish can be sent back to his own people?

I think that the 64 oz, extra-strength can of 'Off' bug spray may be cause for concern. How big are bugs outdoor? Are there free-range bugs able to grow unmolested into something the size of a town car?

I'm worried about bears that can pull the top off of our car like the lid of a Pringles can just to get to the pretzel and three Skittles the children left wedged in the seat.

If there is a storm and it rains all day, I have grave doubts about how long I can entertain the children by holding a flashlight between my teeth and making shadow puppets on the wall of the tent.

If we are not to disturb the environment, does digging a new dam and banking up the creek next to the campsite count? What can a bored child do since disturbing the environment is his/her job? My husband thinks the children will enjoy bird watching and has purchased high-definition binoculars for each child. The children are convinced they will find poison tree frogs and crocodiles. I'm thinking I should I allow them to sneak Game Boys into their backpacks.

What about that socialite who carried her espresso machine up to Everest? Where can I get one?

Armed with only a copy of *The Manly Man's Guide to the Outdoors* and printouts comparing cook stoves, my husband has assured me that two weeks in the wild will be the vacation of my dreams.

My question is whose dream and which one of us is Miss Behaved?
Signed,
So Many Questions, So Many Other Trips to the City We Could Take

Dear Understandably Panicked,

Another question to ask is, if a husband falls in the forest and no one hears him, what is the statute of limitation?

It is not generally Miss Behaved to camp as campers are very sincere and committed to stretching their vacation dollars by camping because the cost of renting a camp site seems so much cheaper than the cost of a hotel room. They save additional money by not flying anywhere but as you have seen, just the right expensive equipment must be purchased in order to be comfortable outdoors.

Camping always involves a great deal of dirt, along with burned food and straight shots of liquor because someone forgot the mix.

It is the Miss Behaved opinion that if broadband reached deep into the western wilderness, and some sort of 24-hour delivery system was put into place, more Miss Behaved women would camp because we could access bluefly.com at any time, anywhere.

That not yet being the case, the Miss Behaved advice for any woman or sensitive and evolved male considering a family camping trip is— stay indoors.

Tea and Sympathy

Reading Addict

◆

My family members point out that reading is very Miss Behaved, antisocial, and selfish. I acknowledge this even as I reach for another mystery novel. Like the dieter who adores Richard Simmons and believes in his message, but is still drawn into the donut shop every morning, it's a habit I can't give up.

But, being Miss Behaved, I can blame.

It's my parents' fault.

Books and an obsession with reading can be traced directly to my parents. My parents read all the time. They read in bed every night side-by-side. They sat together and read on the breeze-catching back porch in the summer. They read together while sitting cozily around the dining room table in the winter.

My mother reads historical novels and British mysteries. She pulled so many books from our tiny library in town that she frequently lost track of what she had read so she marked the back of the books in pencil with her initials. She recognized other addicts in the community who used this method, "Oh, there's Nancy, and Emily, they've read this too, must be good." As a child I thought one never marked or otherwise hurt books, so the fact that my mother wrote in the back was fairly shocking, but after five suppressed-memory recovery sessions I'm feeling much better.

My father frequented the used bookstore in town. His were not the kind of books found in the library. He favored the straight-to-paperback novels. The covers were kept hidden from us when we were very little. I remember discovering his cache of books in the study and gazing at the fantastic, lurid covers—half-naked women lying face down in a pool of red, a gun somewhere, and a shadowy figure back lit in a doorway.

As a child I was fascinated with these pictures, why were these women dead? And why were they all in some state of undress? More interesting was that, as I grew older, I noticed that the picture on the cover and the copy on the back rarely complimented each other. The cover was of the victim—the woman. The copy on the back spoke only of the adventurous, hard-bitten male. The death was not important; the novels were about the men's adventures after the death. After fifteen dis-cussion-group meetings with my liberated-goddess group I determined that, regardless of the good figure and elegant dress, it's no fun to be the dead victim.

I loved accompanying my father to the used bookstore. It was a tiny shop tucked between an organic restaurant run by hippies, (I myself was not a fan of organic food, my father passed through an organic food phase that included, but was not limited to, whole wheat pasta, brown eggs and cookies made without sugar. I have noticed that spaghetti laden with wheat bran didn't catch on even in the poorest and hungriest countries), and the old Holbrook Hotel, which I am sure was famous during the Gold Rush, but no one paid much attention to it in the late sixties. Except to frequent the bar.

The bookstore didn't have a name, or a sign outside. The window in the front was white with dust and obscured by stacks of books. Bookshelves of all different sizes created a maze through the tiny store. The shelves reached up so high I couldn't even see the books on the top shelves. Dad took his books up to the front counter, located in the back of the store, and, as far as I could tell, like my mother, traded them for more of the same.

While he chose from the stacks, I was allowed to wander around flipping through stacks of ancient (fifties) fashion magazines and browsing for those books with murdered women on the cover.

I remember it being always summer. The shop was warm and my father always took longer than a child thought necessary. In the close confines of the bookshelves it was easy to work up a sweat. By the time he was ready to leave, I had put away my prejudice against organic food long enough to lobby for a Seven-Up next door. But in a voice that I would channel later, my father told me I could just as well get a drink of water at the fountain in the parking lot.

I wonder if the bookstore got into my blood, if the dust on the books I surreptitiously pulled from the shelves in order to examine the covers for lurid details was absorbed into my skin and possessed me forever. Is the passion for reading something inherited? Or is it passed down by example, opportunity, and repetition, like religion?

Reading, information, and knowledge were my parent's religion. They felt more intensely about their books, the accumulation of information, and pleasure in words and sentences than they ever conveyed about Jesus or God. And after thirteen sessions with my spiritual advisor I realized that this was the attitude passed down to me.

Instead of deriving comfort from the stained glass in a cathedral or finding peace by walking the maze, I find comfort in books. I like the infinity of a book store, the endless supply of knowledge and information. I am drawn to knowledge that can be seen, felt, and taken home. What nurtures me is a bookstore.

Like churches, there are small bookstores and large bookstores.

Small bookstores have the charm of the village church, nurtured along by the residents, visited once in a while by a lost tourist. Small bookstores carry books that are good for you, like the local church where the preacher knows your name, names the sin, and threatens to tell your parents, which is a far more effective deterrent to sin than three Hail Mary's and two Acts of Contrition.

The staff of a small, independent bookstore not only have passion for their product, they actually read their product. Recommendations of what to read are hand lettered and propped up against the currently favored book. The best sellers are hidden on a back shelf discursively labeled 'Popular Fiction.' The small bookstore employee will take a personal check.

The large chain bookstores are like cathedrals built with the money the villagers were really saving for a new school. These temples offer coffee, scones, and sometimes even Seven-Up on a hot day. The best-sellers are stacked like towers of offerings at the door. The choices are vast and shallow. There is no passion in this church; there is no religion. These stores are cared for by indifferent acolytes, comfortable with the computer and the cash resister, but only passing through this store on their way to the next big gig, perhaps a job that doesn't deal with books at all. They have no recommendations.

I am Miss Behaved enough to like the idea that entire city blocks are devoted to books, no matter what the forum. But Miss Behaved people want to know the difference. So when my BSA (Book Store Anonymous) group asked how to tell the difference between a big chain and a small independent because, for instance, Powells in Portland happens to be a really big bookstore but it's 'small' in attitude and selection, I offered this Miss Behaved system.

Go to the writing section in the bookstore. If you have wandered into one of the large chain bookstores, all the writing books will be devoted to getting published.

If you have lucked into a small independent bookstore, all the writing books will be devoted to writing.

If you want to be very Miss Behaved, go find a clean, well-lit place. And read.

How to Read a Romance

———————◆———————

You do it, your neighbor does it, Miss Behaved women do it, we all do it. One time or another a woman is lured to the back of a large bookstore, or to the front of a small bookstore, or to the tiny general store at the beach that sports one revolving rack of books wedged in against the bait freezer, and she buys a romance book.

Romance. That pink-covered, exotic-setting, brooding-male, happy-ending genre that gets no respect yet at the same time represents the most popular books in the publishing industry. Which indicates to many Miss Behaved women that they are not the only one picking up the odd Harlequin Presents. Perhaps the reason romance books are so popular is that there is perverse Miss Behaved pleasure in believing, at least for half an hour or so, that love does indeed solve everything including financial difficulties and bad skin.

The question is not, to read pink or not to read pink? The Miss Behaved question is, where? We don't see these books out on the street. We don't see titles named *Love's Lost Riot of Grief* out on the beach or in coffee shops, unless the reader has wedged it between the covers of *Easy Cobal Language, Volume III* (and we suspect that is the case). Just exactly where does the Miss Behaved Romance book reader, read her romances?

Locked in the bathroom while the kids fill the dishwasher with Silly Putty, all the while yelling over their shoulders, "Don't worry Mom. We're okay".

Romance heroines rarely have children. If the romance heroine does have a child (and of course it's the hero's and he doesn't know it), that precious child is extremely well-behaved and has never even heard of Silly Putty and probably cannot recant every episode plot of *The Simpson's* since 1993. The romance book child is also relentlessly tailed by the nanny, who savvy Miss Behaved readers know is not the safest element to add to a budding relationship. But the nanny or, better, a sympathetic mother are advantageous as they are always on hand to whisk the child away so the romance heroine can get on with advancing the plot. And you thought the *X-men* were a little over the top.

In the car on the way to the weekly Sunday dinner with the in-laws.

Romance heroines don't have in-laws. (Can't, he doesn't know about the child and not even in fiction does a man admit to his mother he's sleeping around.)

In bed while your precious husband (the one you married without the benefit of a single scene or moment that resembles any of the scenes and moments in any of the last three romance novels you've read) watches another Discovery Channel special on unlocking the mysteries of African anthills. He invariably interrupts you during the best part of your book to point out how truly gross the termite queen looks in a close-up.

Romantic heroes don't watch TV.

On the couch that needs new slipcovers while the same husband is out with the boys.

A true romantic hero never goes out with the boys. He'd rather spend every waking minute with the heroine.

In bed with the flu, while all the children, a few of whom you've never met before, rage outside the bedroom door dropping bits of cherry Popsicles and grinding them into the carpet with their stomping feet while your husband is staying at the Four Seasons in New York.

The romance hero says things like, "Honey, I have to attend a tradeshow in Las Vegas. Do you want to come along and luxuriate at the Canyon Ranch Spa while I work my handsome fingers to the bone?" What you heard before you picked up your book was, "This will be a bitch, and it's too expensive to fly you, and I'm sure there's nothing to do in New York, and we're short 3,000 frequent flyer miles, and you're not looking so hot anyway. You should wear more make-up."

At Burger King.

Romance heroines never eat at Burger King. Romance heroines eat at places like LeCirque or Aqua or L'eau, any place that doesn't sound like food nor offers to supersize anything on the menu for an additional 35 cents.

At Chuck-E-Cheese with the Cyber-Monsters Little League Team immediately after their first victory of the season which also happened to be their final game. To be able to read anything here, you will be forced to hide in the simulated air traffic controller game. It's the only game that is always empty because it's too expensive to play and no one wins except Hank Smith and that's because he used to be an air traffic controller before his break down. Any given Friday evening a Miss Behaved search will reveal a woman hiding in that air controller game, her feet on the steering wheel, reading about love at the spa while studiously ignoring cries of anguish from the next room because someone accidentally threw the team's lucky baseball into the ball pit.

Surreptitiously. Hide the latest Silhouette between the covers of *From Dawn to Decadence* while riding the bus into the city to work.

You know by now romance heroes never take the bus, so, if you were hoping to meet someone romantic, it won't be on the number 14. It would be better to get yourself to L'eau and order something small and hope the nanny doesn't quit before you can meet the man of your dreams.

Miss Behaved women usually recover from such indulgences in time and realize that these books are as fictitious as a celebrity biography. But since indulgence is very Miss Behaved, find a corner of the backyard that has not been dug up for a dirt bike track, imagine you're on the beach in Antigua, and take a break from reality.

It's the Miss Behaved thing to do.

The Miss Behaved Author

◆

Dear Miss Behaved,
I have been a struggling writer all my life and I think that my pile of rejection letters has less to do with my talent and more to do with the fact that I didn't have the right kind of past. For instance, I never made excuses for a perpetually drunken mother; I didn't lie for my abusive father. I didn't do drugs. My parents never considered becoming missionaries to the Congo.

Can a Miss Behaved author grow up in a stable family without an interesting background and still become wealthy and famous, or should I have been raised in a poor Irish home in which one was served shoe leather for breakfast?
Signed,
Rejections Cover my Bathroom Walls

Dear Bathroom,
Your fears are not misplaced; you are truly out of luck.
All successful Miss Behaved books are created from the author's personal history that is so horrible with odds against the author that are so great, it is a miracle the child had the inner resources to survive let alone be able to scribble a few words about it on paper.

Just to reinforce the concept that it's not you, and that talent is no substitute for a juicy background story, here is a Miss Behaved chronicle of the average famous author's rise to fortune.

Famous authors are poor children, either from the inner city, the mountains of Tennessee, or an Indian reservation (excuse us, Designated Grounds for Native Americans, come on down, we're playing Blackjack day and night). As a poor, disadvantaged, student, the soon-to-be-famous writer wore shoes repaired with duct tape and couldn't afford the corrective lenses he so desperately needed.

At the tender age of 16, he wrote an essay about being poor, wearing those shoes, and squinting at the blackboard. Abuses from fellow classmates were thrown in for color. The story was published in the school's literary magazine which, as luck would have it, was read religiously by Coppola, who loved it. (We know what you're thinking. He doesn't read it anymore, so forget it.) Coppola published the story in his magazine the next day. Within the week our poor author was offered a six-figure advance to expand his story into a book.

The now famous writer quickly purchased a house in Mendocino. Five magazine articles (not counting the *Mendocino Beacon*) were written about him and they all included photos of the author standing barefoot on a windswept beach and squinting at the horizon. The now famous author spends the rest of the winter on the coast watching in amazement as the book "writes itself."

A great deal of the advance was spent on new shoes.

The first print was a million books. Reviews described the tale as tragic but lyrical in its description of the poor, white, Native American, inner-city black-experience. The book made the bestseller list on the first day it hit the stores, leap-frogging over everything written by John Grisham.

After six months, the newly famous author is nominated for a Pulitzer and receives a Fulbright Scholarship to Harvard where he can hone his true talents. *Diets and Desserts* magazine does a holiday cover with the author holding kittens wearing little Santa hats. The author gets a makeover and starts up a foundation: Shoes for All Native American Inner City Children Between the Ages of Six and Nine.

The author is exhausted by all the attention but agrees to a book tour. At each signing, the author repeats the amazing story and concludes with the great Miss Behaved author line, "I was really lucky and got published without even realizing it".

Sincere writers longing to be Miss Behaved authors know that no matter who they hear speak, no matter what the theme of the writing work shop, they will hear only a handful of explanations from the famous author.

"I was successful right away."

"No, I never received a rejection letter."

"My book was published forty minutes after the manuscript was completed."

"I just can't explain all this attention for my little book."

"I never dreamed I'd be an author. I always wanted to be a welder but the fame and fortune interfered."

These are important Miss Behaved speeches because there is such a discrepancy between born writers and famous authors.

Born writers, such as our friend with interesting bathroom wallpaper, write because they can't help it. From the day they could grasp a fat orange crayon with their chubby fingers, they have struggled to make words. Over more years than they'd like to admit, they have dutifully mailed and e-mailed countless stories and articles, all rejected. But they write on. They come to lectures and book signings looking for the right answer, the one piece of advice that will propel them from the gloom of rejection to the light of publication.

Famous Miss Behaved authors are supposed to help these struggling authors, but they never do, and that's okay. It's wonderfully Miss Behaved to just repeat over and over, "I was really lucky and successful right away, here are slides of my trip to the North Pole."

This is not, of course a real story. A few famous authors have talent and a few published writers received a rejection or two before blinding good fortune took over their lives and they can now afford a ranch in Carmel. But struggling authors doubt that very much. If it's difficult and frustrating for the struggling author to get published with no hope of success, then published authors must have some secret because it seems so damn simple for them. Which is true: Miss Behaved success never takes much effort.

The Miss Behaved suggestion is that, if you want to be an author and you don't come from a dysfunctional background, make one up. Forget writing about the black underbelly of suburban life. It's been done. Your best bet is to create a terrible life, write about it, and tour the country pretending it's all true. The fabrications will be discovered just as your book is slipping from the bestseller lists and the controversy and mea culpas will sustain sales for another six months.

That's our Miss Behaved suggestion. And never think for a second that a famous author is interested in helping you, the struggling author, and will hand out advice on the perfect query letter or whether to double-space or triple-space your manuscript before sending it to Coppola.

There are only ten spots on best-sellers list. All Miss Behaved authors know that.

Miss Behaved Chicken Soup

◆

When my essay appeared in *Chicken Soup for the Writer's Soul,* I was able to attend a number of book signings. After both experiences I am now a Miss Behaved expert and offer advice on how to manage a book signing.

Things to do at your first book signing:
1. When you arrive at the bookstore, double check to make sure the signing is for your book.
2. Try not to time the release of your very first book with that of JK Rowling's fifth book, because it will be all about Harry.
3. Paint your toenails purple.
4. If you are part of a signing for an anthology and you're sharing the spotlight, be grateful because it's not all about you.
5. If you are part of a signing for an anthology and you're sharing the spotlight, be disappointed because your first experience and brush with fame should be all about you.
6. But then again, if the signing tanks, it won't be because it's all about you.
7. Paint your fingernails smog from Urban Decay just because it's such a great name when someone asks.
8. Wear big elaborate earrings so when it's your turn to sign your book for the nice old ladies from the Del Webb Senior Living

Village, they will remember the earrings even if they never get around to reading your story on page 119.

9. Wear a short dress to show off.

10. Wear a short dress to frighten the fans and help solidify in the minds of the young twenty-somethings at the mall that they will never, ever, grow up to look like hideous you.

11. Know that all the fans who are under thirty are wondering what took you all so long.

12 Make sure you correctly spell the names of the two twenty-something's who bothered to attend the book signing, because you remember when you were twenty-something and publication was just round the corner because your novel was fabulous and based on your life so far, an Amy Tan/ Bret Ellis kind of theme in which you daringly spoke about your mother in unflattering terms. And your own book signing was just weeks away because the manuscript was mailed just last month. And you were certain the publisher will love it and send the galleys to Oprah. And frankly, you wouldn't be caught dead sharing the spotlight with anyone else thank you. And it's okay because, on the face of it, you don't think you want to be twenty-something again and re-live those awful first novels, many drafts of which you threw out last year.

13 Have dinner with a friend before the signing because her support will give you confidence and you don't have to explain about your story one more time. She already knows about the story. Pick a friend who is genuinely happy for you.

14 Get lost driving to the next book signing because you distinctly remember that twenty-five years ago Bird Cage Mall and Sunrise Mall were two separate and competing malls. So the large seven-block long Barnes and Nobel bookstore that you passed by twice couldn't possibly be THE Barnes and Nobel hosting the 12:00 signing because it is clearly in the Birdcage Mall and the directions clearly state that you are supposed to be at the Sunrise Mall.

Give up and call the store. Discover you are wrong and it is all one mall and that's what you get for not allowing people and malls to grow, change, and join together in cooperation.

15 Arrive late so everyone will pay attention to you. Remember, you are wearing those big earrings.

16 Invite your mother and encourage her to bring friends from exercise class and a couple of ladies you've known since birth to your book signing. They will mob the tardy you because they are so relieved they didn't drive all the way to the city for nothing and perhaps you aren't as irresponsible as you were during your unfortunate sophomore year in college.

17 Cheerfully stand and hug and take pictures and give the impression that anyone not standing in line to get your signature is missing something big. Notice this works and a number of people do stand in line behind the boisterous home town crowd. Sign and laugh until the harassed organizer of the event can't stand it anymore and makes you sit down with the rest of the more cooperative authors.

18 Make sure at least one of your mother's friends is old enough not to care much about what people think. This fabulous friend will take great delight in the whole event and will walk around and speak to all the authors, the editors, and the most famous person there, saying loudly "Well, I'm a big fan of *insert your name here*'s work and that's why we drove all the way from *insert the home town here* to the big city just to be here." Which is of course true since you babysat her children for years and always cleaned the kitchen after dinner.

19 Have your mother take you to lunch so you can extend the attention for another hour or so.

20 Point out the toe nail polish.

21 Secure promises that they'll attend the next signing because the attention is quite fun and you're ready to do it again. Even if you have to write your own book to do it.

22 As long as the bookstore resides in a mall you recognize.

Fifteen Minutes of Fame

———————— ◆ ————————

Dear Miss Behaved,

My best friend recently informed me that his one minute on Nightline trumps my five minutes on New Channel 50. I quickly countered with reminding him that my 13 months as a radio co-host easily beat his four mentions in the *Chronicle* as "an informed source." Then he insisted that his profile in the *Guardian* had higher point value than my profile in the *Press Democrat* to which I retorted that it certainly did not as my profile was three columns with a photo and his was only two columns with a pull quote.

Are there rules for the fifteen-minutes-of-fame race? Are we terribly Miss Behaved for running this race in the first place? That aside, how will we know who won?

Signed,

Running Behind

Dear Behind,

Many Miss Behaved people are obsessed with becoming famous. Nothing less than a profile in *People* magazine and a walk on part on *ER* will do. In this country the pursuit of fame often supersedes actually accomplishing anything, so we applaud your Miss Behaved efforts. But what is the scoring system? What exactly counts in the fifteen-minutes-of-fame race?

Like Radio station DJs who constantly dream up Miss Behaved stunts in order to get mentioned in the papers, and like those same newspapers who staunchly refuse to print radio call-letters to avoid giving away advertising no matter how truly stupid the stunt was (TPing the Golden Gate Bridge comes to mind), the fifteen-minute-of-fame race can be tricky and subjective. Do you win if the stunt gets in the news? Or do you lose because it's attributed to "some local radio station" that pulled this "damaging stunt"? You lose: no name, no fame.

The biggest and quickest payoffs in the fame game are in television. However, waving to Mom while carted off in the police van after a particularly satisfying protest march because it was a lovely afternoon and you didn't want to attend your political economic theory class anyway doesn't count. Being arrested on TV, even if it's *COPS*, does not add any seconds of fame because your face is always pixilated for 'legal' reasons.

If you are a witness on a televised trial, it counts for a full five minutes of fame, but you must prevaricate and your hair must look good.

Being saved by a TV evangelist does not count.

If you can contract a mysterious and undiagnosed illness, get interviewed by a concerned reporter, and are videotaped walking slowly down a sidewalk covered with fall leaves with a voice-over describing your situation in tragic overtones, it counts for five minutes. If the story is expanded (ripped from the headlines is a good Miss Behaved method of idea generation), and shown as a two-part miniseries, you get ten minutes, but the show must mention your real name.

Receiving an award counts if it is televised. Since most are, this is not difficult. The number of awards corresponds to the number of minutes of fame gained. Seven Grammys equal seven minutes of fame. If you are named "Best New" in any category, give a long acceptance speech. This may be your only chance to gain minutes. The only awards that aren't televised but do gain an often overlooked feature of the pursuit of fame; longevity, are the Nobel and Pulitzer Prizes. In the right group, a

National Book Award would carry some fame points, but only two minutes in the best of situations.

Playing a victim on TV and being shot and killed in the opening sequence has the same point value as being a contestant on one of those Miss Behaved Spring Break programs on MTV where young things write words on hard body surfaces in red lipstick. You must look good in a thong swimsuit to get any points at all; we don't consider being famous for cellulite as a desirable outcome. There are no minutes awarded for just being a member of a Spring Break crowd. But we appreciate the effort with the beer and all.

Game show contestant is a very good way to pick up fame with little cost and only a modicum of talent. If you lose in the first round: 30 seconds of fame. Win repeatedly, three and a half minutes.

If you are crowned homecoming queen and your picture is featured in the local paper, with the crown, it's worth about a minute. To gain an additional three minutes of fame, you must publish a bitter autobiography in your forties about how being queen didn't make your life any better.

Web sites do not count, even if you land on the listserve from Yahoo! Geocities and thirteen more people visit your site devoted to the paraphernalia of President Lincoln's early years, including ash and splinters from the log cabin that is also available on eBay. Too many people are doing this kind of thing. To earn fame seconds, you must stand out from the crowd.

A published book counts for 30 seconds; a self-published book does not count at all.

Signing up to be an extra in a movie shoot does not count. Being hired to be an extra in a movie shoot in which you are named "third palace guard from the left", or "second Klingon warrior from the right", gets you 30 seconds, mostly because you are still unrecognizable, but your name is listed in the credits. If you are listed as "hysterical woman in pink" and your face can be clearly seen, you get bragging rights for as long as the movie is in theaters and 45 seconds of fame points.

If you are a minor public figure and you create some sort of political firestorm by publicly uttering an inflammatory comment that has no bearing on reality but is controversial with a touch of nerve, and the firestorm gets you a cover on *Newsweek* titled "Who the Hell Does She Think She Is?" we'll tell you, she is famous and has ten minutes of fame to her credit.

Sudden fame can trump all previous work and win the game.

If you commit some horrendous crime against man, nature, or small woodland creatures, are convicted in a front-page headline decision, vindicated by Dr. Laura on the radio, and then apologize on TV with Stone Phillips, this counts for the full monty. In fact it's one of the more popular ways to gain fame. The more heinous the crime, the more minutes can be gathered up. This of course is a personal choice and the lifetime incarceration must be weighed against the glory of the moment. But some feel this is worthwhile.

Lucky participation in a fad like *Big Brother* and *Survivor* gain their full allotment. If even the losers from these shows can score a table at French Laundry, they have not only reached the pinnacle of American aspiration, they are also finished with the game. What they do with the rest of their obscure lives is up to them. (Note: just scoring a table at French Laundry can bring in up to 45 seconds of fame depending on day and time).

Seven minutes on Oprah counts for fourteen fame minutes and wins the game. You knew that was coming.

Twelve-Step Program for Writers

◆

Dear Miss Behaved,

I am a writer. But I've never been published. I'm a VP with a prestigious consulting company, I'm married and have lovely children and a well-kept lawn. But still I want to write. What should I do? Is there something else that can replace the meaning and pleasure I get from searching the dictionary for over an hour in pursuit of the perfect word? Is there a technique that would help me stay away from the writer's section of the bookstore? I'm thinking that it would be much easier on everyone in my life if I find a hobby that is more cheerful and, as a side benefit, produces lovely Christmas gifts.

Signed,

Writing This during Lunch Break

Dear Store Bought Christmas,

What is a writer to do? You've attended the seminars; you know that only the truly downtrodden or spectacularly lucky make the bestseller list. How can you wrest yourself away from this damaging sideline you've nurtured all of your life? Many have tried, but Miss Behaved attempts to convince writers that their day job really is important and that it's okay to stop attending seminars and perhaps learn how to cook or shape topiaries instead have failed miserably.

True writers are Miss Behaved; they will never change no matter how much evidence is presented by loved ones that they are pursuing a futile dream. Sometimes the best Miss Behaved way to cope with such a damaging compulsion is to simply accept this and, in some cases, move on to a state of healing understanding and compassionate conservatism. Which is why we have a twelve-step program just for you.

But first a Miss Behaved disclaimer. We are not talking to or about authors. Authors (see famous Miss Behaved Authors for a description) who already have advances and interviews with *Good Morning America*. Real writers often are not published but write despite consistent rejections. Miss Behaved writers write because writing comes from something so deeply ingrained that no amount of superficial hobby projects can suppress the impulse.

This is why you need the Miss Behaved Twelve-Step Program for Unrepentant Writers

1   We admit we are powerless over the compulsion to write. We know that without writing our lives would not only be unmanageable, but unimaginative as well. That without some kind of writing we would bore family members to death with our musings that are often safer confined in the hard drive. We admit that even if it means waking at 5:00 AM in the morning because that's the only time we have, the perfection of language is worth every minute.

2   We believe that a Muse greater than ourselves can restore our creativity and our sanity if we listen.

3   We made a decision long ago to turn our will and our lives over to the care of the Muse as we understand it. Following her guidance, we accept our true inner genre and lyric strengths.

4 We will make a searching and fearless moral inventory of ourselves. We will admit that our novel is boring, our How-To inadequate, our web site a tangle of broken links. We know that the only way to fix any of this is to evaluate the merits of our work, get an outside opinion, then promise to revise.

5 Admit to our Muse, to ourselves and to another human being, preferably another writer since we know no one else wants to hear about this, the exact nature of wrongly used plot points and metaphors.

6 We are entirely ready to have the Editor remove all the defects of our syntax without blame or self-aggravation. We will accept the changes from on high with grace and maturity. We will promise ourselves that this graciousness will lead to eventual publication, otherwise the pain is not worth it.

7 Humbly ask the Muse to remove our shortcomings and our overly long Faulknerian sentences.

8 Make a list of all the people we have misrepresented in the name of creative license, and be willing to make amends to them all as soon as we become best-selling authors. Forgive our parents for not leading a more adventurous life or indulging in more dysfunctional relationships. Realize that we will have to write from our own experiences and, yes, imagination.

9 Make direct amends to such people whenever possible except when to do so would injure them or others. We will not write apology notes to former editors because they had to read and reject our early attempts at humor. And we will not send out our successful how-to book to those same stick-in-the-muds who

didn't recognize genius when it floated across their desks the first time. We will not send nasty e-mails to agents who asked us, at the last writer's conference "I'm only looking for Tom Clancy, are you Tom Clancy?"

10   Continue to take character inventory. Are they two-dimensional? Do the names of four minor characters all begin with the letter D? When the development is wrong, promptly admit it and correct it.

11   Seek through prayer and medication to improve our conscious contact with the Muse as we understand her, praying only for knowledge of the Muse's meaning and the strength to get up every morning before the rest of the family does to carry it out.

12   Having had a spiritual awakening as the result of these steps, we will try to carry this message to other writers and to practice these principles in all our workshops and seminars. Because deep in our hearts we know we won't stop attending the workshops and seminars, we know we can't resist purchasing the next Natalie Goldberg book, we know we won't stop compulsively writing on scraps of paper while we wait in line at the bank. There is too much joy in discovering the right word, the perfect turn of phrase. We know we won't stop. Forgive us.

Perfect Cartwheels

———————◆———————

I come, not just from a family of readers, but from a family of voracious devourers, the raptors of the reading set. We tear into books with complete disregard for manners and witnesses, tossing aside the carcasses onto big piles in the study, then the guestroom, then my old bedroom. My mother is holding up part of her house with pilings made of stacked paperbacks.

Since I don't have that kind of room to collect, I recycle. A book has so many words left after I've used it that it seems criminal to waste them. As my mother is fond of saying, "there's still some good left in them." And I want to share, or as my brother is fond of saying, "because you have to".

As I was roaming the aisles of my favorite used bookstore; trading a bag of bones for fresh meat, I discovered a used book that I had eyed new a few years ago but didn't purchase. Delighted, I picked it up and dropped it in my bag.

The book, *Cartwheels on the Fault line*, is a regional book of short essays, fiction, and poetry that reflect the experiences of the women writers from my own home, Sonoma County.

I bought it because the time was right to read about women exploring their options and writing about them. In the introduction, all the contributing authors spoke of how and why they came together in an anthology. It was their chance to allow their authentic voices to come through. They spoke of the stress of not writing what they wanted because of editors, critics, trying to fit in, to make money, and said they were so tired of all that. They longed for wildness and creativity. I admired the authors and I wanted to do the same thing myself. But that wasn't what impressed me about this book.

Inside the front cover was an inscription: *To a wonderful young woman on her graduation.* Signed *"Ms D"* with a smiley face. The date was 1996 and I know it hadn't been in the used bookstore long because I would have noticed it. So let's say the book appeared on the used bookstore shelf around 1999. Three years since the book was given to that wonderful young woman.

It's not difficult to re-create this young recipient since a long time ago I was a young woman just like her.

This girl received this book as one of a pile of graduation gifts given on a June night that turned chilly by nine o'clock and forced guests to retreat inside. She opened the book, looked at the appealing artwork on the cover, and, briefly, because there were parents and peers in the room, scanned the handwritten dedication. Whatever.

The book did not make the first cut on what to take down to college. It languished in her room for three years. By the third summer, her mother could no longer stand the chaos in the room that was supposed to be converted to a sewing room but the family never got around to it until this summer, and said to the young woman, "Do something about that room."

The young woman, between her third and fourth year at the University, rifled through the books on her bedroom shelf and came across this one. As she scanned the introduction, a picture of the con-tributors formed in her head. These authors were very sincere and probably wore comfortable dresses. She imagined they were very old, some even forty. She was not these women.

Finding their voices indeed, the young woman thinks contemptuously. I don't have limitations, I don't need this kind of advice or sentiment. I already found my voice. I received an A on my personal essay in English 205. I know everything and have complete confidence in my skills and the world in general. In fact, I plan to conquer the world as soon as I graduate and nothing will stand in my way.

She knows everything there is to know about men. She's already dated fifteen guys and has had serious relationships with two of them lasting about six months (the equivalent of five years in college time) each. She knows everything about friends, she's kept some, and lost some and is confident she has adequately internalized the lessons.

She knows about life, she took a series of classes in Western Civ. with Philosophy thrown in for good measure and now has a firm grasp of what and why people do what they do, and behave the way they do.

What she doesn't need is the reminder that she will grow old. She definitely does not want to hear that at age 40 or even 50, she will still be wondering what life is all about. You think about life while in high school during long evenings huddled with friends on the beach, sharing a bottle of wine stolen from a parent's cellar. But to consider those questions when you're old, plus adding in all the regrets and mistakes that are possible by then, is too much to contemplate and far too depressing.

Right now she feels confident and invincible and she wants nothing around her to remind her otherwise or to even bring that disturbing concept onto her radar screen.

She dumps the book into the bag that also holds a half dozen Harlequin romances; *The Scarlet Letter* (Was Hester a loser or what? Just move to a new place and pretend your husband died, like duh!), as well as that very weird book by Margaret Atwood. Who are these writers to warn her about life? She needs no warning, she watches *Mad TV* and *UPN*, she is of the opinion that Jack and Rose should have snatched a place on a lifeboat when they had the chance.

She takes the books to the used bookstore her mother recommends and gets credit but doesn't redeem it. Too much reading in college, she doesn't need to do anymore for pleasure she plans to rent movies and read on the Internet. She wants an e-book for Christmas.

The abandoned book of questions and desires languishes on the shelf until I'm ready to discover it. Which is right and the way it should be. The best way to face life is to do it fresh every time.

And then later reinvent the cartwheel.

Cartwheels on the Fault Line, works by 27 Sonoma County Women, collected by Barbara L Baer & Maureen Jennings, Floreant Press, Forestville, CA

Dear Miss Behaved,
Do Miss Behaved people live longer or is that just my imagination?
Signed,
Confused

Dear Probably Caring for an Old Aunt,
Miss Behaved relatives do live longer. They live longer than anyone or anything else on the planet. Miss Behaved relatives live so long that they sometimes drive previously nice people to commit Miss Behaved acts involving toasters and the bath.

If you too want to live past your uselessness and become a burden to your ungrateful children, the Miss Behaved program of longevity is:

- smoke cigars
- drink high balls
- make loud statements at parties that include "I'm 92 and I always start my day with a big plate of steak and eggs."

The nastier and more difficult a relative is, the longer they live. If you stand to inherit money from the aforementioned Miss Behaved relative, the odds are good that you will perish in a car accident long before they perish from clogged arteries.

Or bad eggs.

To learn more about being Miss Behaved

◆

visit www.missbehaved.com.

About the Author

◆

Catharine Bramkamp lives in Sonoma County and has a background in video and radio production, freelance writing and experience as an on-air radio personality where she learned the important business model; it is easier to beg forgiveness than ask for permission. She has a BA in English Literature from UC Santa Barbara and has published over 300 newspaper and magazine articles. She has appeared most recently in *Chicken Soup for the Writer's Soul* (page 119). Many of the Miss Behaved essays were published during her three years as a weekly columnist for a local paper.